About This Course

You want to create and maintain web pages for your website. The fundamental elements of a web page are HTML, XHTML, CSS, and some JavaScript. These technologies take some time to master. In this course, you will use Adobe Dreamweaver to create web pages while focusing on the content, styling, and design. As you construct the web pages, Dreamweaver will competently create the XHTML, CSS and JavaScript required.

You will also maintain and administer your website with Dreamweaver's site and page management tools. The website and pages you create will reflect your content and design and will be professionally accurate for your site visitors.

The course covers the Adobe Web Communication using Dreamweaver CS6 objectives completely and can be used to help prepare students to take the Adobe Certified Associate (ACA) exam. This course is also designed to cover the Adobe Certified Expert (ACE) exam objectives.

Course Description

Target Student

This course is most valuable for individuals who have been given responsibilities to create or maintain a website. It will also be valuable for new web designers, web developers, and graphic artists who want to extend their skills in creating complete websites. Learning how to use Dreamweaver CS6 will enable the practitioner to create web pages and sites in the most efficient manner.

Course Prerequisites

To ensure success in this course, you should have basic personal computing skills. To obtain this level of knowledge and skill, it is recommended that you first take the following Logical Operations course (or have equivalent knowledge): Introduction to Personal Computers Using Windows 7. For accelerated learning and deeper understanding of this course, it is also recommended that you have some exposure to various web design technologies, so you may also want to take the Web Design with XHTML, HTML and CSS: Part 1 course.

Course Objectives

In this course, you will use Dreamweaver CS6 to design, build, maintain, and upload websites.

You will:

- Identify the capabilities of Dreamweaver CS6, the elements of design, and the technologies used in website production.
- Describe the work and project planning required to create a website.
- Create web pages and content elements for those pages.

- Use Cascading Style Sheets (CSS) to style page content.
- Insert images and manage the image properties.
- Create tables and import external content for the pages.
- Create reusable web assets and page templates for other web pages.
- Generate four types of links used in websites.
- Conduct tests on the website and upload single pages, groups of pages, or entire websites to your Internet Service Provider (ISP) or your web server.

The LogicalCHOICE Home Screen

http://www.lo-choice.com

The LogicalCHOICE Home screen is your entry point to the LogicalCHOICE learning experience, of which this course manual is only one part. Visit the LogicalCHOICE Course screen both during and after class to make use of the world of support and instructional resources that make up the LogicalCHOICE experience.

Log-on and access information for your LogicalCHOICE environment will be provided with your class experience. On the LogicalCHOICE Home screen, you can access the LogicalCHOICE Course screens for your specific courses.

Each LogicalCHOICE Course screen will give you access to the following resources:

- eBook: an interactive electronic version of the printed book for your course.
- LearnTOs: brief animated components that enhance and extend the classroom learning experience.

Depending on the nature of your course and the choices of your learning provider, the LogicalCHOICE Course screen may also include access to elements such as:

- The interactive eBook.
- Social media resources that enable you to collaborate with others in the learning community using professional communications sites such as LinkedIn or microblogging tools such as Twitter.
- Checklists with useful post-class reference information.
- Any course files you will download.
- The course assessment.
- Notices from the LogicalCHOICE administrator.
- Virtual labs, for remote access to the technical environment for your course.
- Your personal whiteboard for sketches and notes.
- Newsletters and other communications from your learning provider.
- Mentoring services.
- A link to the website of your training provider.
- The LogicalCHOICE store.

Visit your LogicalCHOICE Home screen often to connect, communicate, and extend your learning experience!

How to Use This Book

As You Learn

This book is divided into lessons and topics, covering a subject or a set of related subjects. In most cases, lessons are arranged in order of increasing proficiency.

The results-oriented topics include relevant and supporting information you need to master the content. Each topic has various types of activities designed to enable you to practice the guidelines and procedures as well as to solidify your understanding of the informational material presented in the course. Procedures and guidelines are presented in a concise fashion along with activities and discussions. Information is provided for reference and reflection in such a way as to facilitate understanding and practice.

Data files for various activities as well as other supporting files for the course are available by download from the LogicalCHOICE Course screen. In addition to sample data for the course exercises, the course files may contain media components to enhance your learning and additional reference materials for use both during and after the course.

At the back of the book, you will find a glossary of the definitions of the terms and concepts used throughout the course. You will also find an index to assist in locating information within the instructional components of the book.

As You Review

Any method of instruction is only as effective as the time and effort you, the student, are willing to invest in it. In addition, some of the information that you learn in class may not be important to you immediately, but it may become important later. For this reason, we encourage you to spend some time reviewing the content of the course after your time in the classroom.

As a Reference

The organization and layout of this book make it an easy-to-use resource for future reference. Taking advantage of the glossary, index, and table of contents, you can use this book as a first source of definitions, background information, and summaries.

Course Icons

Watch throughout the material for these visual cues:

Icon	Description
	A **Note** provides additional information, guidance, or hints about a topic or task.
	A **Caution** helps make you aware of places where you need to be particularly careful with your actions, settings, or decisions so that you can be sure to get the desired results of an activity or task.
	LearnTO notes show you where an associated LearnTO is particularly relevant to the content. Access LearnTOs from your LogicalCHOICE Course screen.
	Checklists provide job aids you can use after class as a reference to performing skills back on the job. Access checklists from your LogicalCHOICE Course screen.
	Social notes remind you to check your LogicalCHOICE Course screen for opportunities to interact with the LogicalCHOICE community using social media.
	Notes Pages are intentionally left blank for you to write on.

1 | Getting Started with Dreamweaver

Lesson Time: 30 minutes

Lesson Objectives

In this lesson, you will:

- Identify how the World Wide Web works.

- Name the essential design and content components for web pages.

- Locate and use the Dreamweaver interface elements.

- Utilize Dreamweaver Help efficiently.

Lesson Introduction

Dreamweaver allows practitioners at any level to develop websites and web pages with ease and enthusiasm. More than ever, the competition of millions of other websites demands that emphasis must be paid to useful content and innovative design in order to bring interested users to the website.

To use Dreamweaver effectively, you need both an understanding of the fundamentals of the World Wide Web and web page design, and also an understanding of the capabilities and functions of Dreamweaver itself. The skills and information presented in this lesson will give you a foundation to build on as you begin designing websites with Dreamweaver.

TOPIC A

Web Basics

The World Wide Web (WWW) is a global resource made up of millions of websites. These sites are hosted by powerful computers called *servers*. These servers are connected by a dedicated backbone of telephone circuits to our computers and mobile devices, providing us access to the websites on the WWW.

How the WWW Works

To access a website, the user either types or selects a text-based web address called a domain name address. The *Domain Name Service (DNS)*, an Internet utility, translates the text-based domain name address into the numerical address used by computers, the *Internet Protocol (IP) address*. The IP address is used to identify and locate the computer system hosting the website requested. The IP address serves the same role as the typical telephone number you use to call a friend.

When the web server receives the request, it sends the home page of the website to the requesting computer following the path along the telephone circuit that the IP request followed. All of this occurs in a few seconds or less.

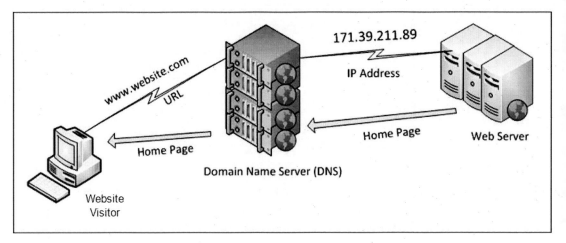

Figure 1-1: Requesting and receiving web pages.

The URL

The *Uniform Resource Locator (URL)* describes the complete address of the website you wish to visit. It consists of several parts all designed to enable the web server to locate the specific web page requested. Forward slashes are used to separate the elements of the URL.

Consider the following URL:

http://www.nga.gov/highlights/index.shtm

- **http://** – the protocol or communications technology to be used. This protocol represents "hypertext transfer protocol." Others that can be used are "ftp://" or "file transfer protocol" and "https://" or "hypertext transfer protocol with a secure connection."
- **www** – a server name. Although "www" has been used almost universally, other server names can appear, such as "msdn," "blogs." "en," and "itunes."
- **nga.gov** – the domain name address of the website. It is this name that is translated by the DNS into an IP address before locating the web server hosting the site. For example, the domain

"google.com" will be changed by the DNS to an IP address, which might look something like "72.14.207.99.".

- **/ highlights /** –the name (and location) of an actual folder on the web server holding web content.
- **index.shtm** – the name (and location) of the web page the browser will open. Although most pages have an "htm" or "html" file extension, which indicates standard, static construction, web pages may have "asp," "jsp," "php," or other extensions depending on the technology used on the page. In this case, "shtm" indicates that the web page is making use of a server side include. A server side include is a scripted instruction stored on the web server to be used on multiple pages.

The IP Address

The Internet Protocol (IP) address is the location of a website. The DNS translates the text URL into the IP address so it can locate the site. The numbers refer to the machine on which the site is hosted.

When the IP scheme was created, the Internet and the WWW were in their middle years of growth and it was thought that the current set of numbers, characterized as Internet Protocol version 4 (IPv4) was sufficient to allow future growth. Unfortunately, the existing set of numbers was depleted in 2011. Anticipating future requirements for IP addresses, Internet Protocol version 6 was adopted in 1995.

The current common IP address contains four sets of numbers ranging from 0 to 255 and separated by dots. A typical IP address number would be: 134.11.231.111. The newer IPv6 IP addresses, now being used, are much more complex but will provide sufficient growth of networks and machines for the foreseeable future. They typically appear as: 2001:db8:0:1234:0:567:8:1.

HTML and XHTML: The Language of Web Pages

HyperText Markup Language (HTML) is the language used on early web pages. It was revised regularly to add capability and functionality to the pages. In its latest iteration, it is dubbed *eXtensible HyperText Markup Language (XHTML)* because it adopted rules of syntax from *eXtensible Markup Language (XML)*, a more rigorously defined language. XML is in widespread and common use today to identify and transfer data to and from applications, computers, servers, and other destinations.

A markup language uses tags to label and identify content. In HTML, tags are used to label content. In many cases, HTML tags also address how the content is to be formatted and presented. One of the main concerns leading to the adoption of XHTML was to separate content from presentation. The purpose today for XHTML tags is that they determine content only, with presentation controlled by Cascading Style Sheets (CSS).

XHTML Characteristics

Because HTML needed to be enhanced, the modifications to HTML were encapsulated in the following rules for XHTML:

- Documents must be well-formed (as defined below). This creates more robust documents than when using the former HTML standards.
- All tags must be closed. HTML tags, which normally do not have a closing tag, are referred to as an "empty" tag. They must use a closing tag or simulate closing with a space (optional) and a forward slash (mandatory). The line break tag (<br>) must be closed by using it in this form:
- All attribute values in tags must be quoted. Example: <a id="nav" href="index.html">
- All tag and attribute names must be lowercase in order to be valid. HTML is case-insensitive.
- All tags must be properly nested. Example: <p><strong>This is text.</strong></p>

Anatomy of a Website

When you view a well-crafted website page, you might see an attractive layout with pleasing colors. There may be a few images carefully placed with supporting information nearby. Another area of the page will have useful information in an easily read format. Elsewhere you might see a navigation bar enabling you to migrate to other pages in the site. In all, it was easy to get around, it was well-constructed, and the information was useful to you.

Such a web page is not an accident. Successful websites consist of carefully planned elements brought together by the trained web practitioner. The web browser plays an important role in assembling the components of the page for the viewer but the page needs to consist of those elements that are useful, interesting, and visibly appealing.

Assembling the material for web pages requires consideration of purpose, planning, design, thought, and creation. All of these endeavors require time and sometimes special skills. In the discussion below, you examine these elements of preparation and how to manage them.

Website Fundamentals

What are the fundamentals so important to website production and how do you assemble them?

Content

Web pages need to display information useful to the web visitor. You cannot begin to create that information without thinking about what will hold the interest of the visitor. In considering content, think about what to include. Be sure to include contact information. Consider if background or history information should be included. What form should the material take? Web pages can be constructed with tables, lists, or narrative. Which information is enhanced with these various forms? Should the site be instructional or informative? Determine what information exists and what information has to be prepared. Is anyone particularly skilled in writing that can help prepare the content? Do not underestimate the time it takes to write good content.

Graphics

Images always brighten up a web page. There is nothing like a well-designed banner at the top of a web page to invite the visitor to spend some time on the website. Do you have a graphic you can use for that? Does a logo exist that can be used on the website? Are there photos of activities that can be used? Should you use standard buttons to link pages or can you create some interesting graphic images? Do you need a subtle texture as a background for your pages? Do you know someone with graphic skills who can create some of the graphic elements you need? Can you buy graphics, and will that be cost-effective?

Graphics enhance web pages. Be sure all the graphics used are stored in a graphics or assets folder in the root website folder. Dreamweaver helps ensure that is done by having us create the site folders before beginning work.

Navigation

Links to other content in your site are what keep your visitors at your site. Be sure your navigation links are easy to find and use. Place the principle navigation links in the upper part of your page (the part the user sees upon getting to the page). Include your logo or a design element that represents you, your purpose, or your business in a prominent place on the page. Have it link to your home page. Secondary links are usually placed in a side bar or at the bottom of the page. Repeat links to important pages with both text and graphic links. Make it easier for your visitor by placing primary and secondary links in the same location on your various pages.

Consider using a duplicate set of navigation links in your footer. Even if you use text links at the top, the duplication is still helpful. You want to make it as easy as possible for people to find the content they are looking for on your site.

Site Map

Create a site map for visitors to your site. Also create a link to it so visitors can find content more readily. A site map is a structured list of all pages in a website listing every page in your site in hierarchical format. It shows the relationship of primary pages and their links to secondary pages for the entire site. It is a valuable aid for the user to find information.

TOPIC B

The Dreamweaver Interface

Becoming adept at creating websites requires a number of skills. Using Dreamweaver is only one of those skills. Mastering Dreamweaver is a priority so you can begin creating web pages quickly and deftly.

All of the elements in the Dreamweaver interface were designed to place useful information and choices at the user's disposal. Making the choices and moving on to the next element is the workflow most helpful to creating websites efficiently. This topic will help you get to know the various interface elements and how they help you create and modify web pages.

The Welcome Screen

The *Welcome Screen* is first seen when Dreamweaver opens. It contains the links to all possible next steps in creating a website.

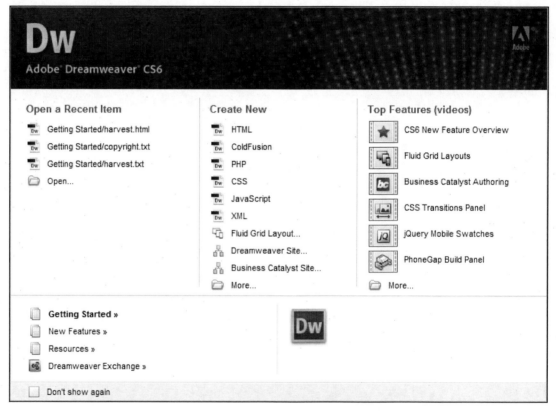

Figure 1-2: The Welcome Screen.

In the **Open a Recent Item** column, you can return to a file in which you worked before or you can open a Dreamweaver-associated file which has never been opened in Dreamweaver. With the **Create New** column, you have choices to create new sites and pages for HTML, CSS styles, JavaScript, XML, or for a variety of web technologies used to create data-driven dynamic pages.

The third column offers links to a variety of video tutorials about Dreamweaver CS6 and its new features. The lower left of the Welcome Screen features links to the Dreamweaver Developer Center, a What's New Center, Help, Tutorials, and the Dreamweaver Exchange, which provides number of add-ons for Dreamweaver.

The Dreamweaver Workspace

The *Dreamweaver workspace* is where you get your work done. It consists of the document that you are creating or modifying and all of the menus, toolbars, and panels used to do your work.

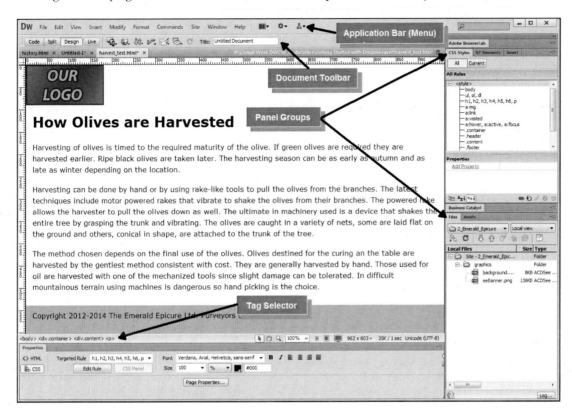

Figure 1-3: The Dreamweaver workspace.

The Application Bar

The *Application bar* contains Windows menu commands as well as the **Workspace** drop-down menu and a search box, providing access to all of the tools, dialog boxes, procedural choices, effects, page elements, and commands available in Dreamweaver. Many of the operations you control by using the **Application** bar can also be controlled by using the panels. Dreamweaver provides multiple places in the **Application** bar and in the panels to access commonly used commands, giving you the option to determine which you prefer as your skill improves.

Figure 1-4: The Application bar.

Most of the menus in the **Application** bar focus on the web page, but two very important choices, **File** and **Site**, give you the tools to create and manage websites and the various files needed to contribute to a well-organized site. The **Window** menu enables you to locate and manage the various panels that occupy the workspace. It also contains commands to arrange and view multiple documents.

There are three icons on the **Application** bar. The **Layout** icon has choices to split the document window into code and **Design** views in various ways. The **Extend Dreamweaver** icon gives you access to Dreamweaver extensions and widgets. With the **Site** icon, you can control, manage, and create new websites.

The Document Window

The document window is the focus of the Dreamweaver workspace. It contains the web page document, scroll bars if warranted, a document toolbar at the top, and a status bar at the bottom. The document window, when maximized, will have a tab in the upper left region with the document file name and a **Close** button.

If the document is not maximized, it will reside within the document area as a document in a moveable, sizable window with a common title bar as its top edge. The title bar will have the full path and file name of the document. The **Document** toolbar, however, will be attached to the **Application** bar.

Two very important features of the document window are the **Document** toolbar and the **Tag Selector**.

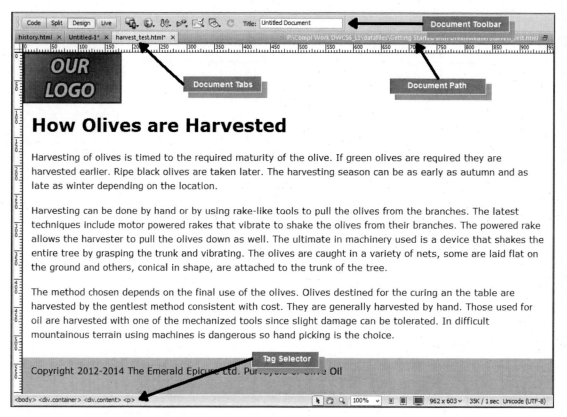

Figure 1-5: The document window.

The Document Toolbar

You use the **Document** toolbar to switch among the **Design** view of the page, which is essentially how it looks in the browser, the **Code** view, in which you can see and modify the instructions for the browser, and the Split view, which assigns a portion of the screen to both views. In Split view, the location of the insertion point is synchronized so you can focus on the same position of the page in Design and **Code** views. The **Document** toolbar also contains a **Live** button, providing a Live view closer to what the browser will render. It does not replace the browser view.

Figure 1-6: The View buttons on the Document toolbar.

The **Document** toolbar also contains other useful buttons.

Document Toolbar Buttons	Description
	Multiscreen icon providing views rendering the current page in the formats of other devices, such as the mobile phone, tablet, and computer monitor.
	Preview/Debug in Browser icon to see the current page in a browser of your choice.
	File Management icon with commands to manage files from and to the web server.
	W3C Validation icon with commands to validate documents to the World Wide Web Consortium standards.
	Check Browser Compatibility icon to check your page HTML or XHTML for support with selected browsers.
	Visual Aids icon to view or hide invisible page elements to mark their location and presence. These markers help identify page components that have no visible display.
	Refresh icon to refresh the page after making code or CSS changes.
Title: Untitled Document	**Document Title** box to enter or edit the page title.

> **Note:** For more information about viewing a web page using different devices, check out the LearnTO **View a Web Page in Multiple Device Formats** presentation by clicking the **LearnTO** tile on your LogicalCHOICE Course screen.

The Properties Panel

The **Properties** panel is also referred to as the **Properties Inspector**. It is usually placed at the bottom of the screen below the open document window. If it is not present on the screen, it can be opened by selecting **Window→Properties** from the **Application** bar.

The purpose of the **Properties** panel is to display the characteristics or attributes of the page element most recently chosen or highlighted. By choosing a page element and setting the contextual options with the attributes of that element in the **Properties** panel, you can control how the element is affected and displayed.

Figure 1-7: The Properties panel.

The **Properties** panel has two levels of attributes accessed by a small white triangle in the lower right corner. In addition, with current standards calling for separation of content and styling, the **Properties** panel contains two buttons at the left-hand side of the upper section: the **HTML** button for selecting content attributes and the **CSS** button for selecting styling attributes.

For example, if you highlight a paragraph of text, the **HTML** button will display the attributes of the paragraph including confirmation of the HTML tag used, its class name or ID, and any indents applied. The **CSS** button will display its font family, size, color, alignment, and any targeted style. It will also display buttons to access the **CSS** panel and for editing the style rules.

Highlighting images, tables, and other elements in the page will display appropriate attributes in the **Properties** panel. This makes for ease in controlling content and styling.

The Tag Selector

The **Tag Selector** is located in the status bar below the document window. It displays the hierarchy of HTML content tags from the location of the insertion point out to the tags that form the page itself. Its purpose is to help select page objects for editing and occasionally to edit or remove a tag.

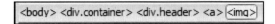

Figure 1-8: The Tag Selector.

The **Tag Selector** is particularly useful in selecting the components of complex objects such as divs and tables, especially table rows and table cells. By pointing to a tag in the **Tag Selector**, you can read any class name or ID assigned to that object. In addition, by reading the tags from right to left, you will see the order of tags that contain other tags. Selecting a tag selects the object on the page.

Panels and Panel Groups

All of the tools required to create the website are contained in the **Application** bar choices and the more accessible panels and panel groups. Panels are used to place objects on a page and to edit and modify the objects as well.

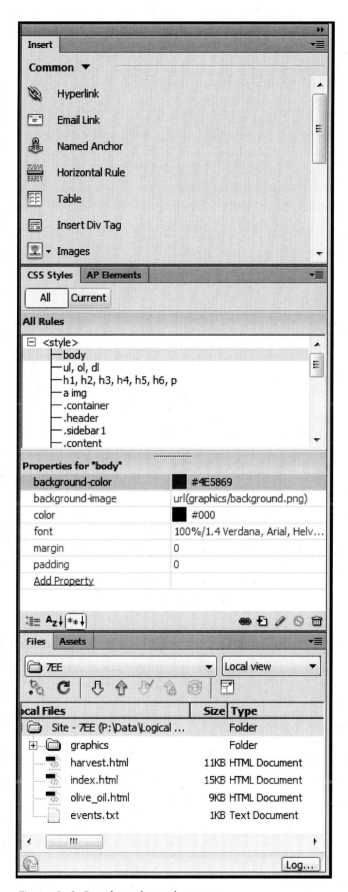

Figure 1–9: Panels and panel groups.

For editing and modification purposes, a panel provides the choices related to the selected object on the page. All panels collapse when their tab is double-clicked, providing more space for another panel or the open document. The panels open for use when the tab is clicked once.

The upper and lower dark grey edge of each panel can be dragged to provide additional vertical space for a panel. Many panels have icons at the top and along their bottom or left edge which you use for additional functionality. Some panels also have buttons to change views or initiate an action.

Panels can be displayed alone or in panel groups. Logically related panels may be grouped for efficient workflow. For example, the **File** panel and the **Asset** panel are generally grouped with tabs providing access to each panel. Panels are generally docked to one side of the screen with the exception of the **Properties** panel, which is generally displayed at the bottom of the screen.

The user can dock, undock, form, and break up panel groups as required. However, it is suggested that the panels be left in place until familiarity with Dreamweaver is attained. Two very important and highly accessed panels are the **Insert** panel and the **Files** panel.

The Insert Panel

The **Insert** panel is one of the more versatile panels in Dreamweaver. It is used to create and place objects on the web page. The objects are grouped into nine categories.

Insert Category	Objects to Insert
Common	Hyperlinks, rules, tables, divs, images, media, widgets, dates, server-side includes, comments, head elements, scripts, templates, tag chooser for various technologies.
Layout	Various divs, Spry (JavaScript) panels, menu bars, accordions, tables, table rows and columns.
Forms	All objects required for forms, Spry (JavaScript) validated form objects.
Data	Data access and display objects, Spry (JavaScript) data and display objects.
Spry	All of the Spry (JavaScript) objects in one place.
jQuery Mobile	A full choice of objects based on the popular jQuery JavaScript framework. Web designers and developers can create mobile application interfaces quickly with consistency.
InContext Editing	Two objects for adding editable regions to templates.
Text	A full selection of HTML tags for direct insertion into a web page.
Favorites	A blank list in which users place their most-used Insert objects. Right-click the text, select **Customize Favorites**, select objects from the various categories, move them to the **Favorite Objects** box, and select **OK**.

Figure 1-10: The Insert panel with the Common category shown.

The Files Panel

The **Files** panel is the command center for managing the files that make up the website. The panel contains two buttons near the top. The left button chooses the directory in the computer to be displayed in the **Files** panel. When you are working in a website, the web root folder should be chosen. The button on the right chooses the view of the files on the local computer or the various servers to which a connection should be made. The server choices include the **Remote Server**, **Testing Server**, and a **Repository** site.

The **Files** panel also provides icons for various management functions.

Icon	Function
	Connection to Remote Server – Not Connected
	Connection to Remote Server – Connected
	Refresh File List
	Get Document(s) from the Remote Server
	Put Document(s) onto the Remote Server

Icon	Function
	Check Out Document(s) from the Remote Server
	Check In Document(s) to the Remote Server
	Synchronize Document(s) between Local Computer and Remote Server
	Expand the View to Display Files on Both the Local Computer and the Remote Server

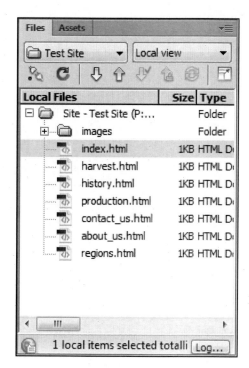

Figure 1-11: The Files panel showing a test site on the local computer.

The <div> Tag

In current practice most web pages are constructed by using the HTML tag <div>. The term "div" is an abbreviation of the word division. With <div> tags, you can block out the various regions of the page in which you place content. A <div> tag denotes a block of space on the page with a specific or variable height and width. Although a <div> tag is a portion of a web page, it functions similarly to the page itself. Any content can be placed in a <div> tag and it expands to fit the content. It can hold text, graphics, tables, or any combination.

The main purpose of a <div> tag is to enable styling and control of the space it occupies using CSS styles. You establish control by giving the <div> tag a unique ID or class name and by setting CSS styles and physical properties to be applied to that ID or class by the browser.

Page layouts generally begin with a <div> tag that represents the entire page. It is commonly given the ID or class "container." Then additional <div> tags are constructed inside the container <div> to hold a banner, sidebars, main content, and footer.

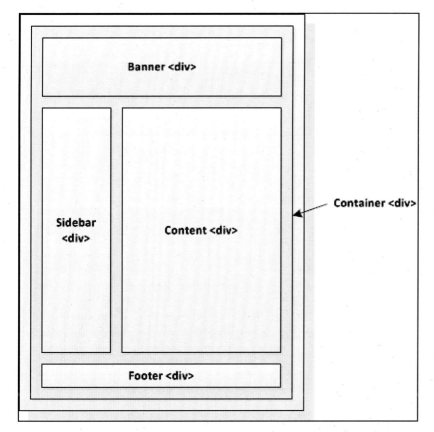

Figure 1-12: A typical page layout using HTML <div> elements.

AP Div

An Absolutely Positioned (AP) element is defined by sheer position and accurate dimensions. It is an HTML element that can contain text, graphics, and any other page element. An AP element can be placed or positioned wherever required on a web page. It can be placed in front of other AP elements or behind them. The visibility of AP elements can also be controlled. Each AP element is given a unique name and stacking order. The boundary of an AP element is gray in color and it is not visible when viewed in a browser.

 Access the Checklist tile on your LogicalCHOICE course screen for reference information and job aids on How to Use the Document Toolbar

 Access the Checklist tile on your LogicalCHOICE course screen for reference information and job aids on How to Use the Tag Selector

ACTIVITY 1-1
Using the Document Toolbar and Tag Selector

Data File

harvest_test.html

Scenario

Your company, Emerald Epicure Ltd. is a new importer, distributor, and seller of olive oils and other products derived from olives from around the world. The president has asked that a website be constructed to announce the new company to the world. You are the person responsible for creating the website.

The marketing manager decided to create a sample page for the site dealing with olive harvesting. She suggested that you look at it and use it for the site if you think it is appropriate. You want to review the page and some of the visual aids available on the **Document** toolbar to better understand the construction of the harvest.html page, which uses a Dreamweaver layout. Additionally, you would like to clean up some of the extraneous tags the marketing manager said she left on the page.

1. View and explore the sample web page.
   a) Select **Start→All Programs→Adobe Dreamweaver CS6** to open the Adobe Dreamweaver application.
   b) Close the **Help Improve Adobe's Products** dialog box, if present.
   c) On the **Welcome Screen**, at the bottom of the **Open a Recent Item** section, select the **Open** button.
   d) In the **Open** dialog box, navigate to the **C:\092001Data\Getting Started with Dreamweaver** folder.
   e) Select **harvest_test.html** and select **Open**.

2. View Visual Aids.
   a) On the **Document** toolbar, select the **Visual Aids** button.
   b) Note the number of visual aids that are checked.

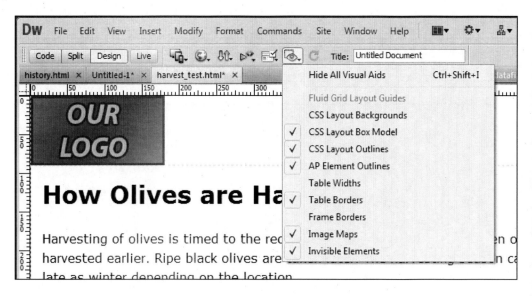

   c) Also note that the header and footer areas have dotted lines delineating their upper and lower limits.

    d) Select **Visual Aids→CSS Layout Outlines** to turn off the **CSS Layout Outlines**.

    e) Note that the dotted lines denoting the header and footer sections are no longer displayed.

    f) Select **Visual Aids→CSS Layout Backgrounds.**

    g) Note that each section of the document displays a bright color. Each color identifies a separate portion of the page defined by <div> tags.

    h) Select **Visual Aids→Hide All Visual Aids**. The page does not display any extraneous marks or colors.

    i) Select **Visual Aids→Hide All Visual Aids**. All of the default visual aids are turned on again.

    j) Select **Visual Aids→CSS Layout Backgrounds**.

    k) Note that the bright colors disappear.

3. Identify page sections with the **Tag Selector**.

    a) Place the insertion point in a blank area of the header section.

    b) Note the rightmost tag in the **Tag Selector**. It indicates the insertion point is in the <div> tag area with a class name of header (<div.header>)

    c) Place the insertion point in a blank area of the footer section.

    d) Note the second from the right tag in the **Tag Selector**. It indicates the insertion point is in the <div> tag area with a class name of footer (<div.footer>)

    e) Place the insertion point somewhere in the text of the first paragraph.

    f) Note that the rightmost tag in the **Tag Selector** indicates the text in the location of the insertion point is in a paragraph tag <p>.

    g) Note the second from the right tag in the **Tag Selector**. It indicates the insertion point is in a paragraph tag <p> within the <div> tag area with a class name of content (<div.content>).

4. Remove tags with the **Tag Selector**.

    a) Place the insertion point immediately above the footer.

    b) Note the rightmost tag <h2> in the **Tag Selector**. This is an unused, empty tag with no content.

    c) Right-click the **<h2>** tag.

    d) Select **Remove Tag**.

    e) Save the document as *my_harvest_test.html*

    f) If an update links window pops up, select **Yes**.

    g) Close the open files, but keep Dreamweaver open.

TOPIC C

The Elements of Web Design

Constructing a successful website requires a complete set of working elements. These elements provide the content for the user and ease of navigation throughout the site. You have visited sites that were pleasing and full of useful information. Just as likely, you have also been to sites that were confusing and lacking in noteworthy subject matter.

Every visit to a website can be a research experience. In addition to searching for information, you can determine what you like about the site and what could be improved. In this way you can establish your design sense and confirm what works and what doesn't. Knowing the difference can help you build a solid and popular site.

Best Practice Web Design

When planning your website, you should consider how you will provide a suitable user experience, what worthwhile content to include and how to construct interaction and navigation that is understandable and easy to accomplish. The best designers consider every element in the website from the standpoint of how it contributes desired content for the user. Providing content is paramount.

There are other considerations as well. All principles of web design contribute to the content. Is it presented well? Is it easy to find? Is the page layout confusing? Do the colors contribute or detract from the content? Several basic principles emphasize the fundamental concept of content delivery.

Fundamental Design Principles

Most designers agree that the fundamental design principles below should be applied to every website. Design principles are always considered when planning a new site. However, websites evolve and target audiences tend to change. When it is time to review an older site's appearance and purpose, these principles should be reviewed. It is generally good practice to continually reexamine the site in light of these principles to keep the site focused on its intended purpose.

 Note: There is agreement that all of these design principles are essential to successful websites. They are included here as suggestions to be included in construction of a website. They should be given careful consideration. Some of the topics are beyond the scope of this course and should be researched independently.

Design Principles	Notes
Target audience	Who are you trying to reach? (family, friends, children, adults, a community, professionals, consumers, businesses, folks with a common interest)
Site purpose	Is the site's purpose to inform, gather information, provide a service, sell a product, explore an issue, inform people about you, or comment on the news?
Content	What content will be presented? Will you originate it or will it be republished information?
	What aspects and subtext of the content will be included?
	In what form will it be presented? (lists, tables, or narrative)
Page layouts	Should the layout adjust to screen resolutions?

Design Principles	Notes
	Will some pages use a banner, footer, or sidebars?
Graphics	Will the graphics be business-oriented, for children, colorful, or conservative?
	What photos will be used?
	Do the graphics exist?
	If not, who will prepare them?
Colors	Consider the colors that reinforce the theme and content.
	Certain colors convey a traditional quality and other colors present a whimsical and playful mood.
	Color choices and reactions to them are usually personal.
White space	White space is the area on a web page that contains no content. When used appropriately, it helps to reduce clutter. Web pages that appear cluttered make it difficult to find information.
Navigation	Navigation to other pages and sites should be logical, understandable, and easy to use.
	Choose the navigation location and pages on which they should be placed.
	Determine the look and feel of the navigational elements (text links, graphics links, rollover effects, and special buttons).
Site map	Create a site map, a list of pages contained in the website.
	The site map is invaluable to visitors looking for information.
	It is also accessible to search engines.
	Consider including an alphabetical list of information available on the site.
Feedback	Users expect a visual response when the mouse pointer hovers over choices on web pages.
	The better websites use these devices to help the user make choices.
	Rollovers, pop-ups, and suddenly visible elements enhance the web experience. Consider including an About Us page, a Contact Us page, a Services page, and a Successes page. These pages complete your story and give the user a way to contact you.
Marketing plan and search engine optimization	New websites are not found readily. Publicize your website. Research the many methods for attracting attention to your site. Use all means accessible and available. Learn to optimize your site for the search engines. You will build traffic and ensure your site's success.
Web metrics	Data can be collected on user visits to your site.
	Measurement, collection, analysis, and reporting of that data is done to assess and improve the effectiveness of a website.
	Research how to see that data.

Colors

Colors can be selected wherever there is a color picker box 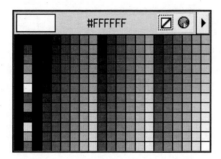 in Dreamweaver. The colors offered are the *216 Web Safe colors*. Web Safe colors were necessary many years ago when monitors and graphics cards did not have the capability of displaying all colors smoothly. Today's equipment is capable of displaying 16.7 million colors and you are no longer limited to choosing one of the 216 Web Safe colors.

Figure 1-13: Dreamweaver's 216 Web Safe colors.

In the HTML environment, colors are specified by using a hash or pound sign (#) and six digits from the hexadecimal system. For example, #23CC88 produces a medium blue-green color. The hexadecimal system of numbering allows six digits to describe 16.7 million colors instead of eight digits as would be required in the default decimal system you use for everyday numbers. In the hexadecimal system, the numbers range from 0 to F, passing through the first six letters of the alphabet after the numeral 9. Therefore, counting up in the hex system would be 0, 1, 2, 3, 4, 5, 6, 7, 8, 9, A, B, C, D, E, F. You can say that A represents the number 10 and F the number 15.

The numbers also have very special significance depending where they are placed in the color number itself. For example, the first two digits represent the amount of red color. Lower numbers such as 23 or 45 indicate lower and darker red content. Higher numbers such as CA or DE represent higher and brighter red content. The same is true for the second set of two digits, which represent the green content. The last two digits are the blue content.

When the numbers are all the same, such as #CCCCCC, the color is a level of gray. The "gray" colors run from #000000 black (no color) to #FFFFFF, which is white (maximum color). Numbers that have repeating color numbers such as #AA3399 can be abbreviated as #A39 because the browser can make the translation.

Use of Color

How Many Colors?

This question does not have a hard and fast answer. In general, one can say that the risk of using too many colors is greater than the risk of using too few.

Too many colors will make the page distracting and busy. It usually makes it harder for the viewer to find the information he or she wants. It is also more tiring to the eyes.

A page with too few colors, on the other hand, risks being a bit boring, but this need not always be the case.

One commonly used rule in these matters is to use three colors.

- **Primary color:** This is the main color of the page. It will occupy most of the area and set the tone for the design as a whole.
- **Secondary color:** This is the color on the page to "back up" the primary color. It is usually a color that is close or analogous to the primary color.

- **Highlight color:** This is a color that is used to emphasize certain parts of the page. It is usually a color that contrasts more with the primary and secondary colors, and as such, it should be used with moderation. It is common to use a complimentary or split-complimentary color for this.

Page Layouts and Colors

Choosing a layout for a web page can be daunting. Designers are guided by the content to be placed on the page. Dreamweaver supplies layouts that can be used for most pages. Many of them include styling and instructions for their use. To save time, you might want to try a layout that will provide the appropriate space for your content.

Color is another matter. Most web practitioners will use colors dictated by their client or the organization to which they belong. Usually the company logo will contain colors that are intended to be used for the website. Generally, cooler colors such as whites, blues, greens and grays are used for business sites. These sedate colors will use an occasional brighter color for accent.

Sites oriented toward family or children will naturally use much brighter colors for attention. Sites depicting art or photographs generally use deep grays or black to emphasize the colors of the art and photos. Color is always a personal choice, but it should be evaluated by other members of your group.

 Access the Checklist tile on your LogicalCHOICE course screen for reference information and job aids on How to Find Page Layouts and Colors

 Access the Checklist tile on your LogicalCHOICE course screen for reference information and job aids on How to Choose Colors

ACTIVITY 1-2
Finding Page Layouts and Colors

Data Files

harvest.txt

copyright.txt

OurLogo.jpg

Before You Begin

Dreamweaver is open.

Scenario

You want to create your own version of the olive harvest page. You want to use a Dreamweaver layout to save time in constructing page areas for the content and graphics you intend to use.

1. Choose a layout.
    a) Select **File→New**.
    b) In the **New Document** dialog box:
        1. Select **Blank Page** from the first column.
        2. From the **Page Type** column, select **HTML**.
        3. From the **Layout** column, select **1 column, fixed, centered, header and footer**.
        4. Select the **Create** button.

2. Insert a graphic.
    a) Place the insertion point to the right of the **Insert_logo** area at the top of the page.
    b) In the **Application** bar, select **Insert→Image**.
    c) Navigate to the **C:\092001Data\Getting Started with Dreamweaver\graphics** folder.
    d) Select the **OurLogo.jpg** file and select **OK**.
    e) In the **Dreamweaver** message dialog box, select **OK**.
    f) In the **Image Tag Accessibility Attributes** dialog box, select **OK**.
    g) Select the **Insert_logo** area in the upper-left corner of the page, above the inserted graphic.
    h) Press **Delete**.

3. Remove unwanted color.
    a) Select the olive green area to the right of the logo you placed by clicking on its lower edge.
    b) In the **CSS Styles** panel, ensure that the **Current** button is selected.
    c) In the **Summary for Selection** area, select the **background-color** style rule.
    d) Select the **Edit Rule** [✐] icon at the bottom of the panel.
    e) In the **CSS Rule definition for .header**, from the **Category** box, select **Background**.
    f) In the **Background-color** text box, enter the color **#FFF**
    g) Select **OK**. Note that the header background is now white.

4. Add text content.
    a) Select the title "Instructions."
    b) Type *How Olives Are Harvested*
    c) Highlight all the body text under the title and press **Delete** to delete it all.

d) In the **Application** bar, select **File→Open**.

e) In the **Open** dialog box, navigate to the **C:\092001Data\Getting Started with Dreamweaver** folder.

f) Select the file **harvest.txt** and select **Open**.

g) In the **Application** bar select **Edit→Select All** and then select **Edit→Copy**.

h) Select **File→Close** to close the **harvest.txt** file.

i) Select **Edit→Paste** to place the text on your page after the title.

5. Complete the footer.

a) In the **Footer** area at the bottom of the page, select the text **Footer**.

b) In the **Application** bar select **File→Open**.

c) In the **Open** dialog box, navigate to the **C:\092001Data\Getting Started with Dreamweaver** folder.

d) Select the file **copyright.txt** and select **Open**.

e) In the **Application** bar, select **Edit→Select All** and then select **Edit→Copy**.

f) Select **File→Close** to close the **copyright.txt** file.

g) Select **Edit→Paste** to place the text on your page.

6. Choose a color for the footer from the logo.

a) Place the insertion point in the footer after the word "Oils."

b) In the **Tag Selector** below the document, select **<div.footer>**.

c) Scroll up until you can see the header.

d) In the **CSS Styles** panel, select the color swatch for the **background-color**.

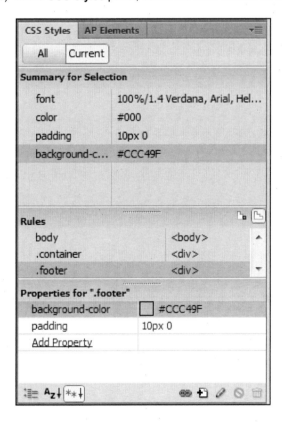

e) Bring the color eye dropper up to the logo and choose the yellow color in the logo letters.

f) Choose a blank area of the page to deselect all.

7. Save the page and view in a browser.

a) On the **Application** bar, select **File→Save As**.

b) In the **Save As** dialog box, navigate to the **C:\092001Data\Getting Started with Dreamweaver** folder.

c) Type the file name *my_harvest.html* and select **Save**.

d) If a graphic warning box pops up, select **Copy**.

e) To check the page in a browser, in the **Document** bar, select the **Preview/Debug in Browser** icon.

f) Select **Preview in IExplore**.

g) View the preview, and then close the browser.

h) On the **Application** bar, select **File→Close** to close the page.

TOPIC D

Dreamweaver Help

Dreamweaver Help draws on many sources in order to accelerate the web practitioner's skills. Every time you consult Dreamweaver's Help system, you add to your knowledge, understanding, and proficiency.

Accessing Help

Selecting the **Help** menu from the **Application** bar opens access to specific help for many of the technologies used to create web pages. There is access to tutorials, the Dreamweaver Support Center, and Adobe Forums, where experiences with Dreamweaver is shared by others. There is also access to multiple text references for the technologies used in web pages.

Dreamweaver Help opens a comprehensive world of help aids. It is a gateway to assistance and tutorials on a variety of subjects. A search box also facilitates queries into specific subjects or procedures.

The References

Choosing **Help** and then **References** will open a Reference panel with access to 13 detailed reference texts on the technologies used in web production. Ten of the references are published by the O'Reilly organization. These resources make Dreamweaver a self-contained resource for web production.

 Access the Checklist tile on your LogicalCHOICE course screen for reference information and job aids on How to Use Help

ACTIVITY 1-3
Using Help and Accessing the References

Before You Begin
Dreamweaver is open.

Scenario
You understand why Help is useful for confirming how to perform various procedures and learning about Dreamweaver. You want to check it out for some of the latest news on Dreamweaver CS6 about workspaces and workflow. Additionally, you have never used the references in Dreamweaver and you would like to check out the CSS Reference.

1. Check out Help in Dreamweaver CS6.
   a) On the **Application** bar, select **Help**.
   b) Select **Dreamweaver Help**.
   c) From the subjects listed at the top, select **Workspace and workflow**.
   d) Under **Workspace and workflow**, click the **Dreamweaver workflow and workspace** link. In the next page, select the **Document window overview** link.
   e) Note the comprehensive discussion of each element and the subsequent discussion and figure of the **Document** toolbar overview.
   f) The detailed descriptions for each choice on the **Document** window will help you become familiar with their function.
   g) Close the browser.

2. Check the built-in CSS style reference.
   a) On the **Application** bar, select **Help→Reference**.
   b) Select the **Book** drop-down arrow.
   c) Select the **O'REILLY CSS Reference**.

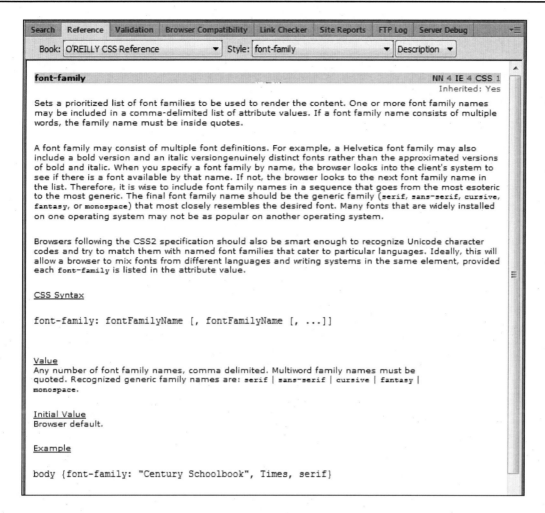

d) Select the **Style** drop-down arrow.
e) Select **font-family**.
f) Note the complete discussion of the font-family style.

g) Select the **Panel Option Menu** button 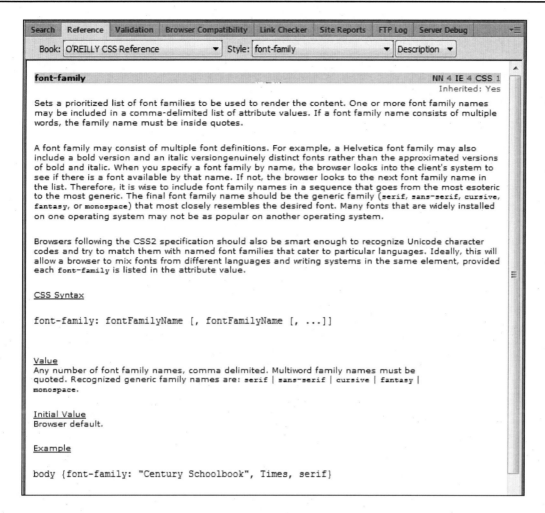 (upper right) for the **Reference panel**.
h) Select **Close Tab Group**.

Summary

In this lesson, you learned how the World Wide Web operates so you can better craft your website. You learned the components to use to create a successful website. You can now utilize the major components of the Dreamweaver interface in your workflow. This brings you closer to creating sites and pages quickly and effectively. You also saw how to use Dreamweaver Help to accelerate your proficiency.

What are the most important considerations in creating a website for yourself or your organization?

Where's a good place to find color combinations to use on your website?

 Note: Check your LogicalCHOICE Course screen for opportunities to interact with your classmates, peers, and the larger LogicalCHOICE online community about the topics covered in this course or other topics you are interested in. From the Course screen you can also access available resources for a more continuous learning experience.

2 | Creating a Website

Lesson Time: 20 minutes

Lesson Objectives

In this lesson, you will:

- Plan the website project.
- Use design tools to plan the site.
- Set up the website in Dreamweaver.

Lesson Introduction

Creating a website means more than producing some web pages and linking them together. Some existing sites require refurbishing. Others require a complete plan from concept to realization of the site.

Planning the site and the work necessary to complete it should be the first step. Because you already know that visitors to your site are looking for useful information, you must be sure that your plan includes all of the information you wish to display, the time you estimate it should take, and the resources you will use to accomplish all of this.

Estimates of the work to be done and who will do it are particularly important. Therefore, organizing the site and the work necessary to create it should be your next task. You need to know what tools are available for planning the work.

TOPIC A

Plan the Website Project

Planning starts by examining the task and its components. Building a website is not a simple task—many elements make up even the simplest website.

Initiating a Project

New web projects are initiated by a variety of entities. Those entities fall into three groups: families or friends; communities or people who have a common interest; and professionals, consumers, and businesses. A project can be initiated by anyone who needs to communicate information, knowledge, and news about a subject.

In addition to creating a site from scratch, there are times when an existing website's content needs to be revamped. This can come about because information about a group has changed, new products have been added, services or missions need to be communicated, the latest news needs to be reported, or the site seems to have become outdated. This need should be reviewed as often as every six months.

Defining the Site Deliverable

Whether the site is being redone, having a new group of pages added, or being created from scratch, you should apply the same considerations. Identify the content it should contain, the way the content should be arranged, and color and layout options.

Most decisions about the look and feel of the site and the need for additional pages for the site will have important implications for the amount of effort necessary to accomplish the goal. You should be sure to keep in mind what the work entails and who will do it.

The Elements of Work Required

Every element placed on a web page will require some effort. The common components used on typical pages include text, graphics, lists, tables, sections of the page defined by <div> tags, navigation bars, rollover images, image maps, and forms.

Web Page Component	Effort Considerations
Text	Text can be copied from existing publications owned by the organization or created as original content. The effort for original text is considerably greater.
Graphics	Illustrations and photographs can be purchased or originated by the organization. Purchased graphics can be expensive. Some sites offer low-cost or no-cost graphics. Read the terms of use for the no-cost sites carefully.
	Creating illustrations and taking and processing photographs require special skills. Commit to graphics carefully. Anticipate costs and effort.
Lists	Lists require accurate and complete information. Research may be necessary. Creation of a list does not take any appreciable time.
Tables	Tables require the most effort in adjusting for merged and split cells and styling, although constructing basic tables does not take much time.

Web Page Component	Effort Considerations
\<div\> tag sections	Sections of the web page require sizing, location, styling, and ordering of elements included in the sections. Planning, creation, styling, and maintenance for each section will take some effort.
Navigation bars	Navigation bars will take some time from planning to construction. Once created they can be used on multiple pages with ease.
Rollover images	Rollover images require two graphics per rollover. Creation of each is straightforward but will take some time. Consider using a limited number of rollover images.
Image maps	Image maps require a modest amount of time to create. The image map graphic must be created first because it is not likely that an appropriate photo or illustration will be available. Then the hotspots must be drawn, which link to other destinations. Finally, the link destinations are input.
Forms	Forms take the most time. Because they are the devices with which web visitor input is obtained, they must be planned carefully.

Estimating the Duration

After considering the pages you need in your site and the elements you wish to include on the pages, you should consider how long it will take to produce each page. There are two considerations for estimating the duration of the various efforts: (1) Will you do it? (2) Will you ask a colleague or professional to accomplish the task? Keep in mind that some of your requirements for the site require special skills.

Generally, doing the work yourself will take less time but you should consider when you will have time to do it. The duration of a task includes the time you must wait before you can begin and the time to complete the work. In some cases, having a colleague or professional do the work may take less time but may involve some other cost.

Establishing the Sequence of Work

Creating a website does not necessarily require a strict sequence of steps. Although planning should come first, once you have a fairly complete plan, you can start work on any particular page. Generally, the home or index.html page will be the page you begin with because it represents the purpose and look and feel of the entire site. Once the home page is finished, any other page can be started. Some web practitioners do a page at a time and only move onto another page when the current one is complete. Others work in waves placing all the text on the planned pages first and then adding the graphics on all the pages. The method used is not as important as being sure the pages are complete and not missing any elements.

Assigning Resources to Do the Work

If you have the luxury of assigning work to others, be very sure they have the skills and desire to help. The highest level of skill you will need for a basic website is someone who is versed in computer graphics and can create simple illustrations or has some photography and Adobe Photoshop skills.

The large corporate sites usually take advantage of web production skills for hire. Resources working on some corporate sites can include copywriters, editors, designers, photographers, digital learning specialists, accessibility experts, navigation professionals, and color consultants.

 Access the Checklist tile on your LogicalCHOICE course screen for reference information and job aids on How to Plan a Website Project

ACTIVITY 2–1
Defining a Website Project

Scenario

The president of Emerald Epicure Ltd. asked you to plan the site before working on its components. He asked you to take a few minutes to fill in the planning form with your preliminary thoughts about the website. He wants the site to include everything about olives and olive products, including growing, harvesting, processing, and global standards for olive oil.

He reminded you that the company sells olive oil and other products from sources around the world, including Australia, France, Greece, Italy, Portugal, Spain, and the United States. He asked you to be sure to include the olive-oriented vacations, events, and festivals held around the world.

He added that the products the company sells includes olive oil, cured olives, olive paste, olive tapenade, flavored olive oil, olive oil soap, and olive oil–based cosmetics.

Let's discuss completing the Web Project Planning Form for Emerald Epicure Ltd.

a) Choose an item that needs completion and offer some comments about what needs to be considered to complete it.

b) Include in your suggestions if the work for that item can be done in house or must be done by contract professionals.

Component	Notes	Resource (In-house, Contract)
Target Audience	Customers of olive products and olive-related events	In-house
Site Purpose	Information and history of olives and olive products	In-house
Required Content		
Number of Pages		
Required Graphics		
Image Map	Include an image map for olive-oriented events worldwide. Link to specific events	Contract
Rollover Images?		
Required Lists	Types of olives, countries producing olives, and olive products	In-house
Colors	Three main colors to be used. Any additional colors for emphasis and highlighting.	Contract
Navigation Style	Include a navigation bar and links in the footer on each page	In-house
Include Site Map?	Yes, showing all pages and how they are linked	In-house

Component	Notes	Resource (In-house, Contract)
Feedback Form? Include Contact & About Pages?		
Marketing Plan? Search Engine Optimization?		
Web Metrics?		

TOPIC B

Use Design Tools to Plan the Website

The planning you have accomplished thus far is high-level planning. You have determined the general characteristics of the site. Now it is time for you to plan more of the detail. The design tools available for planning the website at this stage are simple and primarily graphic.

Design Tools to Plan the Site

The tools used help you visualize the pages to construct and the general flow of the site.

Planning Tools

Rough sketches of how the site will look are the desired planning tools. Over the years the WWW has been active, various effective means have been invented to visualize a proposed site. The value is they are simple to use and especially easy to revise since you and your colleagues will change your minds about how the site should look from time to time.

Flow Charts

Flow charts are graphic depictions of workflow. Each parcel of work is represented by a rectangle. The chart also shows the sequence of the work. It is used to plan not only the work to be done, but also the sequence in which it should be accomplished. It can be informally sketched or created with flowchart software.

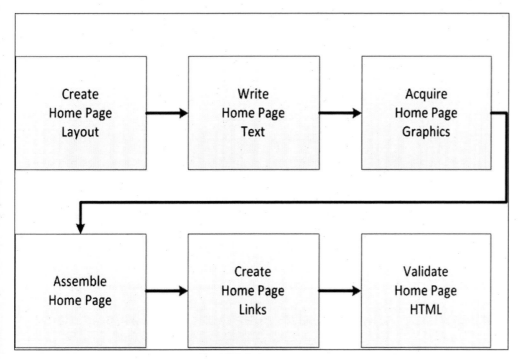

Figure 2–1: A flow chart depicting the creation of the home page.

Wireframes

Wireframes are more detailed planning tools. Wireframing should be done early in the design process. If your site is more than basic, wireframing enables you to clarify exactly what needs to be on each page. If you choose to create a wireframe, you will sketch your page layout in some detail. Some wireframes actually suggest colors to be used, indicate page dimensions, and illustrate where major sections of the page are located. An excellent tool for rapid wireframing and prototyping is Adobe Fireworks, part of the Adobe Creative Suite 6. These design tools are particularly useful when the entire site or portions of it are outsourced to contract professionals. They are helpful as well to define the site for yourself.

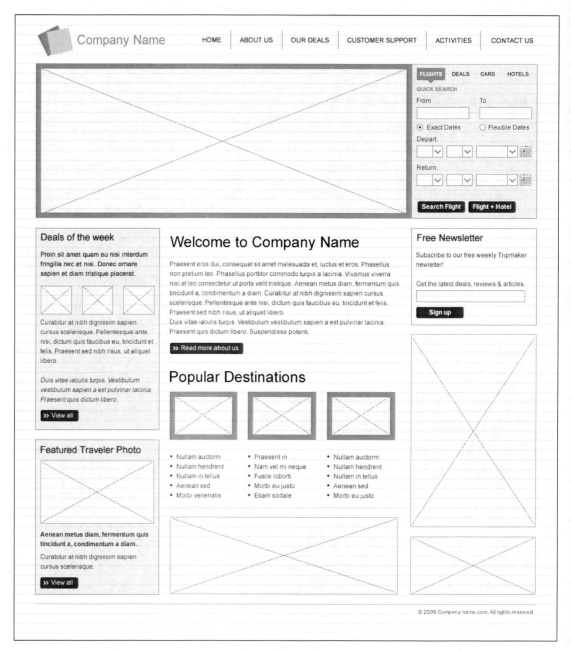

Figure 2-2: A professionally created wireframe for a web page constructed in Adobe Fireworks.

Storyboards

The concept of storyboarding comes from the film industry, where such *storyboards* are used to visually plan each scene in a movie or documentary. In website planning, storyboards are created to show specific page layouts. They are generally sketched by hand and are used to envision the various pages. The great advantage to storyboards is that alternate layouts can be sketched and compared prior to selecting the best one to use for the page.

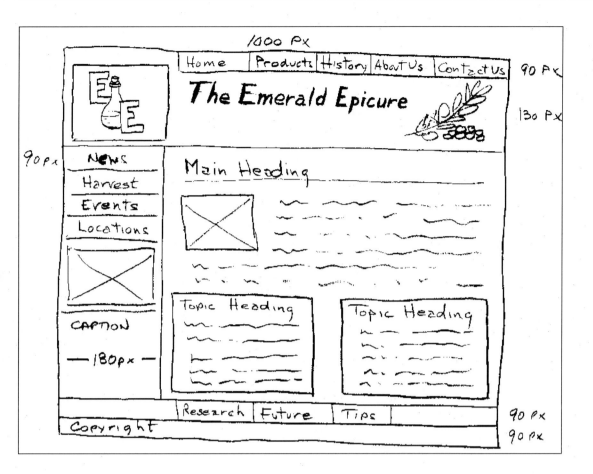

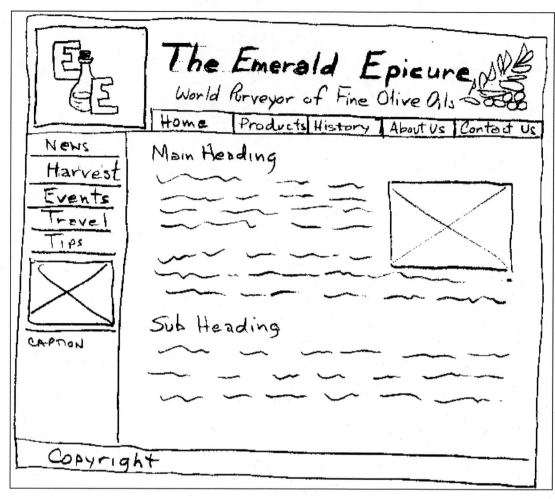

Figure 2-3: Hand-sketched storyboards, one with proposed dimensions.

Site Maps

Site maps are the master plan for the website. They are created and used to plan and construct a new site or a major addition to a site. The site map shows all of the pages and how they are linked to each other. In addition to building the site, the site map is useful for guiding the site visitor through the site's content.

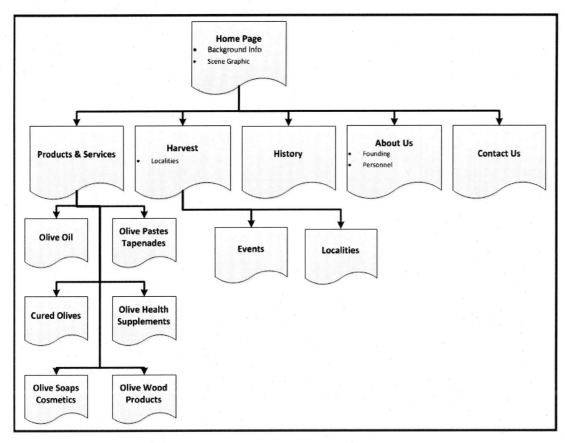

Figure 2-4: A site map.

Project Management

Project management is a discipline applied to a complex deliverable product or result. Being able to anticipate, plan, and document all of the work that needs to be done to create the deliverable is a vital asset. Project management also serves as the documentation in tracking the progress and quality of the work.

When project management is applied to complex projects, the many work details are more effectively controlled. There are four major elements in every project.

Major Project Component	Notes
Work Tasks	The essential work tasks of the project. These tasks will be documented and tracked as to performance and timing.
Durations	The time estimated for each task to be completed, taking into consideration the resources required to complete the task.
Sequence	The order in which the tasks will be done.
Resources	The people, skills, materials, supplies, contractors, professional service, and facilities required to complete the project.

 Access the Checklist tile on your LogicalCHOICE course screen for reference information and job aids on How to Plan a Website Project

ACTIVITY 2-2
Charting the Website

Scenario

The president of Emerald Epicure Ltd. asked you to prepare a preliminary site map for his review. He wants to be sure you will include pages for the major products, events, and history. It's essential that you list as many page ideas as you can, as you can always combine pages if you need to reduce the number of pages later. You will list only page subject/titles in outline form.

By using a word-processing application or creating the site map by hand, you would likely produce something like:

⊕ **Home Page**
    ⊕ **Products and Services**
        ⊖ Olive Oil
        ⊖ Cured Olives
        ⊖ Olive Tapenade
        ⊖ Olive Soaps
        ⊖ Olive Cosmetics
        ⊖ Olive Leaf Tea
    ⊕ **Harvest**
        ⊖ Harvest Events
        ⊖ Localities
    ⊕ **Events and Museums**
        ⊖ Harvest Events
        ⊖ Olive Festivals
        ⊖ Olive Museums
        ⊖ AgriTurist Vacations
    ⊖ **History**
    ⊖ **About Us**
    ⊖ **Contact Us**

---

1. Of all the planning tools discussed, which planning tool do you consider the most important?

2. What components of a website require the most planning?

TOPIC C

Set Up the Website in Dreamweaver

You have planned the site and have a clear idea of what needs to be created. Now you need to set up the site in Dreamweaver so all the elements, pages, and other file components will be saved and stored in a location that Dreamweaver will maintain for the site. Because the storage site is on your computer, it is termed the local site.

Once the site is created in Dreamweaver, all site files stored there will be accessible and supported in the relationships to be eventually sent to the web server. You will save time creating, accessing, editing, and linking the files in Dreamweaver.

Creating the Website Root Folder

It is essential before launching a website project that you set up a site in Dreamweaver. Dreamweaver then helps with link connections and manages all site-wide operations. All of the web files you create will be included in the site root folder available in the local machine. This folder is called the site's local root folder. If you are responsible for more than one website, you will have a local root folder for each website. This allows you to keep the files for each site separate but still accessible.

Basic Site Definition

Establishing a basic site requires only that you identify the site root folder name and location and that you create a graphics folder within the root folder to hold all supporting graphics. When new pages are constructed and linked to other destinations, Dreamweaver will store the page files in the site root folder and maintain the link connections. When graphics are inserted into the pages they will be stored in the graphics folder.

When you are ready to send your completed website to a web server, you will add connection information to your site definition. That includes the server address to which the files will be sent and your ISP account user ID and password to access the web server. Dreamweaver stores this additional information and provides a seamless connection to your server when required so you can send new files to the server and retrieve files for maintenance.

Advanced Site Definition

If your site requires additional instructions to access a database or operate a shopping cart, a testing server can be chosen. The testing server validates programming code written to facilitate dynamic pages that access databases. The programming languages supported are ASP, Cold Fusion, JSP, and PHP MySQL.

 Note: For more information about how to design a web page, check out the LearnTO **Choose a Method of Applying Content to Web Pages** presentation by clicking the **LearnTO** tile on your LogicalCHOICE Course screen.

The Manage Sites Dialog Box

The **Manage Sites** dialog box is the focus for all site functions and procedures. Sites can be created, imported, deleted, edited, duplicated, and exported. Business Catalyst sites, which are built and published using dynamic, built-in modules, can be created and imported through this dialog box.

Note: The Adobe® Business Catalyst® service is a unified hosting platform that enables you to create sites without any server-side coding.

The Role of the Files Panel

When your site is created, the **Files** panel will display your site root folder and any files existing in that folder. From that point on, you can add, delete, rename, and move files and folders to organize the hierarchy of files and folders. With this, a site map can be easily created. The **Files** panel is used to transfer files to and from the remote server. An optional setting enables you to set up a **Check In/Check Out** process to prevent files from being overwritten. This technique is also used to synchronize the files on your local and remote sites.

When you reposition or move files within the root folder, issues relating to broken links are encountered. But when you reposition files within the **Files** panel, broken links can be prevented. The **Files** panel provides an option to check for broken links and displays issues, if any, in the **Link Checker** panel.

Access the Checklist tile on your LogicalCHOICE course screen for reference information and job aids on How to Set Up a Website

ACTIVITY 2–3
Setting Up a Website in Dreamweaver

Before You Begin
Dreamweaver is open.

Scenario
You know you shouldn't begin the construction of the website before setting up the site in Dreamweaver. That requires identifying the location and name of the site root folder and the graphics folder within the root folder. Dreamweaver will then begin maintaining your files and folders as well as monitoring your links.

 Note: The Local Site folder will be identified for each lesson as the folder with the same name as the lesson in the 092001Data folder (see step 2).

1. Name the new site.
   a) On the **Application** bar, select **Site→New Site**.
   b) In the **Site Setup for Unnamed Site** dialog box, in the **Site Name** text box, type the site name you will use for this lesson: *2EE*

2. Identify the site root folder.
   a) To the right of the **Local Site Folder** text box, select the **Browse for folder** icon.
   b) In the **Choose Root Folder** dialog box, navigate to the **C:\092001Data\Creating a Website** folder.
   c) Select **Open** and then select **Select**.

3. Identify the **graphics** folder.
   a) In the **Site Setup for 2EE** dialog box, select **Advanced Settings**.
   b) To the right of the **Default Images folder** text box, select the **Browse for folder** icon.
   c) In the **Creating a Website** folder, select the **graphics** folder.
   d) Select the **Open** button.
   e) Select the **Select** button.

4. Save the site and confirm the listing of the site folders.
   a) In the **Site Setup for 2EE** dialog box, select the **Save** button.
   b) In the **Files** panel, note the site root folder, **Creating a Website** and the **graphics** folder.

5. Dreamweaver needs to know where you will be keeping your files for the website. That folder is called:
   ○ Website folder
   ○ Remote server folder
   ○ Local site folder
   ○ Site files folder

6. The graphics folder holds the images used on the web pages. This folder should be stored:
   ○ On the desktop.
   ○ In the site folder.
   ○ Anywhere.
   ○ On the server.

7. All of the following are considered site planning tools except:
   ○ Storyboards
   ○ Wireframes
   ○ Flow charts
   ○ Dreamweaver

Summary

In this lesson, you planned the site pages and content and reviewed the Dreamweaver planning tools. You have an appreciation of how to estimate the work necessary and you now understand that special skills may be required to help with the site. You set up the site so you can begin work on the actual pages immediately. If the site were a larger endeavor, you would consider employing project management principles.

What planning tool seems to be particularly effective for you?

Is it important to review the skills required for some components of web pages? If so, why?

 Note: Check your LogicalCHOICE Course screen for opportunities to interact with your classmates, peers, and the larger LogicalCHOICE online community about the topics covered in this course or other topics you are interested in. From the Course screen you can also access available resources for a more continuous learning experience.

3 | Creating Web Pages

Lesson Time: 1 hour

Lesson Objectives

In this lesson, you will:

- Create web page documents.
- Add head and text components to a web page.
- Add lists and quotations to a web page.
- Set web page properties.

Lesson Introduction

You have created the root folder for the website. Now it's time to begin creating the web pages for the site. The primary purpose for the site is to share information. Therefore, each page will contain information in an attractive layout, easy to read, with meaningful graphics and navigation components to take the visitor to other sites and other pages.

TOPIC A

Create Web Page Documents

A web page consists of several components, all of which are carefully thought out and planned. They include the layout, colors, structure of the information, graphics, and the navigational elements. All elements contribute to the page and its importance to the viewer.

Typical Page Layouts

Web pages have a discrete number of potential layouts. Typical components used are banner headers, page footers, left or right sidebars, and a main content area.

Banners add a colorful heading to a page. They should include a logo or other interesting graphic that reflects the site purpose.

Page footers end the page but contain additional information. They contain links to pages that might be of secondary interest. They contain a copyright statement and other organizational data.

Sidebars contain more detailed information related to the page topic. The information they hold includes topic details, quotations and graphics.

Basic File Types

Dreamweaver supports creation of pages in different file types. They include HTML, XSLT, ActionScript, CSS, JavaScript, XML, ASP- JavaScript, VBScript, .NET C#, .NET VB, ColdFusion, JSP, and PHP.

Choices for Basic Page Structure

Dreamweaver provides some of the best basic layout choices. The layouts are of two basic types, fixed and liquid. The fixed choices result in a page width that doesn't change with visitor monitors of different resolutions. The liquid layouts can adapt.

Screen Resolutions and Page Sizes

To choose a basic layout for a site requires that you decide how to handle the varying screen resolutions users have around the world. Recent statistics indicate that almost 98% of site visitors have a screen resolution of 1024 pixels wide x 768 pixels high or higher. Only 2% have a screen resolution width of 800 pixels or less. To check on the latest resolution data, visit **www.w3schools.com/browsers/browsers_display.asp**.

If you choose to cover most of the visitor's screen, create your pages at least 975 pixels wide. Only the 2% will be forced to use their scroll bars to see the full width of the page.

If you choose to create pages for all visitors and not adapt the pages to the variations encountered, choose a fixed width layout and make the width 800 pixels or less. Those with higher resolutions may be unhappy with the small web pages they see in their browser.

If you wish to accommodate all current resolutions, choose a liquid layout and set a minimum and maximum width to accommodate the variations.

Choosing a Page Layout

To choose a layout at this point, you must decide if you want just a header and footer, a left or right sidebar, or both. You will most likely choose the header and footer to be on every page. Certain pages will have sidebars for topic emphasis.

Placing lists and tables along with graphics can be done on any page when content is added.

Saving Web Pages

When saving pages, best practices dictate that they be saved with a file extension of .html although .htm is also recognized by Windows, Mac, and Linux operating systems.

File Naming Conventions

File names for pages and graphics should:

- Use simple names.
- Describe the page content or purpose.
- Use all lower case.
- Use no spaces or special characters.
- Use an underscore between words.
- Use "index.html" for the home page.

Organizing Web Files and Folders

With the site root folder named and located, all files and folders will be kept in the folder. Dreamweaver helps maintain the files and folders. The graphics folder is kept in the root folder and all graphics that support the pages will be stored and linked to that location.

Dreamweaver creates other folders when you create special components and stores them in the root folder. They should be left undisturbed because any alteration will result in components not functioning.

The Home Page

The *home page* is the entry point for the visitor to your site and as such it should be inviting, informative, graphically interesting, and have an easy to understand summary of what the site is about. As mentioned earlier, it should be named "index.html" so the browser can choose it as the entrance to the site. The page should also have elements that will invite search engines to list it.

Major Web Page Sections

Every web page consists of two major sections—the head section and the body section.

The head section functions as an administrative part of the page. Most items included in the head section are not seen by the site visitor but they are critically important to the proper functioning of the page.

The head section is defined by the <head></head> tags and includes:

- Declarations – instructions to the web browser about the version of HTML used in the page.
- Meta Tags – various tags are used including those containing key words and page descriptions for search engines and instructions to the browser about redirection and character sets.
- Page Title – the only content in the head section seen by the visitor in the title bar of the web browser.
- CSS Styles – included between <style></style> tags that the browser applies to the page.
- JavaScript Instructions – applied to the page when called to by statements in the body section of the page.

- Links – to separate style sheets and JavaScript pages of instructions for styling and modifying the elements on the page.

Search Engine Considerations

At some point in the creation of each page the content should be reviewed and modified to support search engine listing of the site. Search engines primarily read the text on the page. This includes keywords and description meta tags, text content, alternate text, title text for graphics, captions for graphics, and the document title.

 Access the Checklist tile on your LogicalCHOICE course screen for reference information and job aids on How to Create Web Pages

ACTIVITY 3-1
Creating Web Page Documents

Before You Begin

Dreamweaver is open.

Data Files

ee_banner.png

background.png

Scenario

The president and marketing manager of Emerald Epicure Ltd. would like to see what the home page will look like. You decide to create as complete a page as you can with the graphics you planned to use.

1. Name the new site for this lesson.
   a) On the **Application** bar, select **Site→New Site**.
   b) In the **Site Setup for Unnamed Site** dialog box, in the **Site Name** text box, type the site name, *3EE*

2. Identify the site root folder.

   a) To the right of the **Local Site Folder** text box, select the **Browse for folder** icon.
   b) In the **Choose Root Folder** dialog box, navigate to the **C:\092001Data\Creating Web Pages** folder.
   c) Select **Open** and then select **Select**.

3. Identify the graphics folder.
   a) In the **Site Setup for 3EE** dialog box, select **Advanced Settings**.

   b) To the right of the **Default Images folder** text box, select the **Browse for folder** icon.
   c) Select the graphics folder.
   d) Select **Open**.
   e) Select **Select**.

4. Save the site and confirm the listing of the site folders.
   a) Select the **Save** button.
   b) In the **Files** panel, note the site root folder, **Creating Web Pages** and the **graphics** folder.

5. Select a page layout.

   a) On the **Welcome Screen**, in the **Create New** column, select **More** ⌷ More...
   b) In the **New Document** dialog box, in the first column, confirm that **Blank Page** is selected.
   c) In the **New Document** dialog box, in the **Page Type** column, confirm that **HTML** is selected.
   d) In the **Layout** column, select the **2 column liquid, left sidebar, header and footer** layout.
   e) Select the **Create** button.

6. Prepare the header and insert the header graphic.
   a) Select the **logo placeholder** labeled **Insert _logo (20% x 90)** upper-left element in the header.
   b) Press **Delete** on the keyboard.
   c) Place the insertion point in the **header** section.

    d) To confirm the insertion point is in the header, check the **Properties** panel. Be sure the **HTML** button is selected on the left. Be sure the **Class** text box contains the word **header**.

    e) Select the **Code** button in the **Document** toolbar.

    f) Note the class name **header** for the header **<div>** section.

 Note: Styles in **Code** view are in the page <head> section and in pink characters. The following instruction notes the location of the .header style on or near line 54. If line numbers are not seen in **Code** view, turn them on by selecting the **Line Numbers** icon from the **Code** toolbar (left side of the workspace) in **Code** view.

    g) Scroll up and locate the **background-color** style for **.header** on or near line 54.

    h) Change the color to **#FDF100**.

    i) Select the **Design** button in the **Document** toolbar. Note that the header is now yellow.

    j) Save the page to the C:\092001Data\Creating Web Pages folder as *index.html*

    k) Select the **header** section.

    l) On the **Application** bar, select **Insert→Image**.

    m) Navigate to C:\092001Data\Creating Web Pages\graphics and double-click to select the **ee_banner.png** file.

    n) In the **Image Tag Accessibility Attributes** dialog box, in the **Alternate text** text box, type *The Emerald Epicure Banner*

    o) Select **OK**.

7. Change the page layout background color.

    a) In the **CSS Styles** panel, select the **All** button.

    b) In the **All Rules** section, select the **body** rule.

    c) Select the **background-color** color swatch.

    d) Select the white color in the first column.

8. Change the navigation buttons' layout background color.

    a) Select the navigation button in the sidebar with the text "Link one."

 Note: Make sure you select the button and not the text.

    b) Select the **Current** button at the top of the **CSS Styles Panel**.

    c) Under the **Rules** heading, select the **ul.nav a, ul.nav a:visited** rule.

    d) In the **Properties for** area, select the **background-color** swatch.

    e) From the color swatches, select the white color in the first column.

9. Remove the sidebar layout background color.

    a) In the **CSS Styles** panel, select the **All** button.

    b) In the **All Rules** section, scroll down to the **sidebar1** style listing.

    c) Select the **sidebar1** listing.

    d) In the **Properties for** section, select the **background-color** color swatch.

    e) Select the white color. Note now that the whole sidebar is now white.

    f) Save the document and keep it open.

TOPIC B

Add Head and Text Components to the Page

Head components are administrative elements that generally are not seen by the site visitor. They contain information for the browser and search engines. Other elements are for storage of JavaScript functions that may later be called to run by elements in the body of the page. Styles are also stored in the head section, which the browser utilizes to create the page.

Meta Tags in the Head Section

Meta tags are tags with information about the page that the browser invokes or the search engines read. The most important meta tags are the **Keywords** meta tag and the **Description** meta tag. You will use both to provide important information about the page content for the search engines to add to their database. This information helps direct visitors to your site when they use those words in web searches.

Text in the head section can be original content composed for the website or it can be taken from existing marketing materials and brochures. It is best to keep the information succinct and interesting. Use headings before different topics to describe the nature of the information that follows. Maintain the visitor's interest with relevant graphics, lists, and tables of data.

Page Titles

Page titles are one of the most important elements on the page, especially in Dreamweaver. It is so important that Dreamweaver gives us a **Title** text box in the **Document** toolbar so you won't forget to enter a title for the page you are constructing. The page title appears in the browser tab. If it is left unedited, the default page is automatically titled Untitled Document.

Headings

XHTML and HTML provides six sizes of headings from H1, the largest size signifying the most important heading, to H6, a very small heading indicating the least important. Headings help organize a page and announce changes in information themes. Most pages make use of H1 through H3 headings.

Benefits of Using Appropriate Tags to Contain Text Content

When you use appropriate tags to add text in a web page, it offers you control over the page design. Your task of formatting text becomes easier and a uniform formatting style can be maintained across web pages. For example, when you choose to use the Heading 1 tag (which is available by default in Dreamweaver) for titles, you are able to apply a similar formatting style to all the titles at the click of a mouse button. Similarly, text content that is placed within a Paragraph tag will contain similar font style, size, and space across all pages. This helps in designing consistent looking pages with reduced effort and time.

Situations That Require Inserting Special Characters

When adding a copyright statement or a privacy policy to your web page, you may need to insert special characters such as a copyright symbol (©) or a registered mark (®). These symbols cannot be entered directly from the keyboard, instead they can be inserted on a web page by selecting **Insert→HTML→Special Characters→<required special character>**. Also, Dreamweaver allows only single space between characters because HTML cannot encode multiple spaces. If you want to insert multiple spaces between characters, then you have to insert a non-breaking space HTML code by using . HTML then identifies it as a single entity to encode.

HTML Encoding For Special Characters

The default encoding for the English version of Dreamweaver is Western (Latin 1). The HTML entities for special characters start with an ampersand (&) and end with a semicolon. For example, the HTML entity for copyright symbol (©) is ©

The HTML entity for a special character can also be a series of letters. For example, the HTML entity for copyright symbol (©) can also be © The special characters that are inserted from within Dreamweaver may not be displayed in all browsers and on all platforms, if the web page does not use Western (Latin 1) encoding. It is recommended to test a web page with special characters in different browsers to ensure that the characters appear properly.

Difference Between ‹p› and ‹br› Tags

The ‹p› and ‹br› tags are HTML tags that are used to control the formatting of text content in a web page. The major difference between them includes:

Tag	Function
‹p›	Defines text as a paragraph on the web page. It includes a space at the beginning and end of the paragraph.
‹br›	Inserts a single line break between paragraph tags.

 Access the Checklist tile on your LogicalCHOICE course screen for reference information and job aids on **How to Add Head Content and Text**

ACTIVITY 3-2
Adding Head Elements

Before You Begin
The file index.html is open.

Scenario
The marketing manager wants to be sure you include the olive products Emerald Epicure sells and the fact that the site covers all aspects of olives, from cultivation to harvesting to production. She made a special request to include a short slogan in the title of the home page. You already planned to do all that.

1. Add a **Keywords** meta tag.
   a) On the **Application** bar, select **Window→Insert** to open the **Insert** panel.
   b) In the **Insert** panel, be sure the **category** drop-down option is **Common**.
   c) In the **Common** category, select **Head→Keywords**.
   d) In the **Keywords** dialog box, type *Olives, Olive Oil, Tapenade* and select **OK**.
   e) Select the **Code** button and verify that Dreamweaver added a meta tag with the **name="keywords"** attribute and the **Content** attribute containing the keywords you entered.
   f) Select the **Design** button.

2. Add a **Description** meta tag.
   a) In the **Insert** panel, be sure the category drop-down option is **Common**.
   b) In the **Common** category, select the **Head** drop-down arrow.
   c) From the drop-down menu, select **Description**.
   d) In the **Description** dialog box, type *This site describes the science and lore of olives and olive derived products.* Select **OK**.
   e) Select the **Code** button and verify that Dreamweaver added a meta tag with the **Name="Description"** attribute and the **Content** attribute containing the description you entered.
   f) Select the **Design** button.

3. Add the page title.
   a) In the **Document** toolbar, select the text **Untitled Document** that is in the **Title** text box.
   b) Type *The Emerald Epicure Ltd. Home Page* and press **Enter**.
   c) Select the **Code** button and note that Dreamweaver added the **Title** text you entered between <title> tags in the head section of the page in or about line 5.
   d) Select the **Design** button.
   e) Save your work and preview it in the browser.
   f) Keep **index.html** open for the next activity.

The Document Title

The document title is one of the most important elements on the page. It becomes a description of the page in the URL Address text box and tab of the Web browser. If you forget to complete the page title, the browser will display "Untitled Document" in the URL Address text box and tabs of the Web browser.

ACTIVITY 3-3
Adding Text and Headings

Data File

C:\092001Data\Creating Web Pages\index_page.txt

Before You Begin

The file index.html is open.

Scenario

You understand that the home page is the entry point to the website and you will include text information about all aspects of olives, including the history, cultivation, and production to ensure the visitor's interest in visiting all of the other pages in the site.

1. Create the page heading.
   a) Select the heading "Instructions" at the top of the page.
   b) Type *Olives and Our Lives*
   c) Note that in the **Properties** panel, in the **Format** drop-down menu, that the heading is a **Heading 1**.

2. Add text.
   a) Select all of the remaining text on the page ending with the **Background** heading and the following paragraph and press **Delete**.
   b) In the **Files** panel, double-click the **index_page.txt** file to open it.
   c) On the **Application** bar, select **Edit→Select All**.
   d) Select **Edit→Copy**.
   e) Close the **index_page.txt** file.
   f) Select **Edit→Paste**.
   g) Save your work.

3. Enter the page headings.
   a) Select the text "The Saga of the Olive."
   b) Ensure that, in the **Properties** panel, the **HTML** button is selected.
   c) In the **Format** drop-down menu, select **Heading 2**.
   d) Select the text " History of the Olive."
   e) In the **Format** drop-down menu, select **Heading 3**.
   f) Select the remaining two headings, "Cultivation and Harvest" and "Olive Products" and convert them to **Heading 3**.
   g) Click in another area of the page to deselect the headings.
   h) Save your work and leave the index.html file open for the next activity.

TOPIC C

Add Lists and Quotations

Lists are a convenient way to display information that is logically associated. It presents the material concisely and in an easily read format. You can create a bulleted list (unordered list), a numbered list (ordered list), or a glossary-like list (definition list). In order for the list tags to format the list items appropriately, each list item must be a separate paragraph.

Unordered Lists

Unordered lists are generally termed "bulleted lists." By using HTML attributes, you can choose two types of bullets, circles and squares, by accessing the **List Item** button and selecting the **Style** drop-down arrow in the **Properties** panel.

Ordered Lists

If the list items must be numbered or lettered, an ordered list is required. The selection for numbering is a bit more extensive than the selection of bullets. By accessing the **Style** drop-down list in the **List Properties** dialog box, you can select **Numbers**, **Roman Small**, **Roman Large**, **Alphabet Small**, and **Alphabet Large**.

Definition List

Definition lists are useful for displaying technical terms or text that warrants explanations, additional information, or definitions.

 Access the Checklist tile on your LogicalCHOICE course screen for reference information and job aids on **How to Create Lists**

ACTIVITY 3-4
Creating Unordered and Ordered Lists

Data Files

history.html

u_list.txt

producers.txt

Before You Begin

The file index.html is open.

Scenario

You want to list the various uses for olives in a bulleted list and include it in the sidebar on the home page. You also wish to begin to add content to your page on harvesting olives. In addition to describing the process, you will list the world's leading producers of olives in an ordered list.

---

1. Create an unordered list in the sidebar.
   a) Select the text in the sidebar below the **Link** buttons and press **Delete**.
   b) Type *Uses for Olives*
   c) In the **Properties** panel, be sure the **HTML** button is selected.
   d) Select the **Format** drop-down button and select **Heading 3**.
   e) Place the insertion point immediately after the "Uses for Olives" heading and press **Enter**.
   f) In the **Files** panel, double-click the **u_list.txt** file to open it.
   g) Select and copy all of the text in the **u_list.txt** file.
   h) Close the **u_list.txt** file.
   i) Paste the text into the sidebar.
   j) Select the text beginning with "Stuffed Olives" and ending with "Olive Wood."

   k) In the **Properties** panel, be sure the **HTML** button is selected and select the **Unordered List** icon.
   l) Click in the whitespace of the sidebar to deselect the unordered list.
   m) Save and close **index.html**.

2. Add an ordered list to the sidebar.
   a) In the **Files** panel, select the **history.html** file and right-click it.
   b) Select **Open** from the pop-up menu.
   c) Place your cursor under the **Links** section.
   d) Type *World's Leading* and then hold the **Shift** key and press **Enter**.
   e) Type *Producers of Olives*
   f) In the **Properties** panel, be sure the **HTML** button is selected.
   g) If necessary, select the **Format** drop-down button and select **Heading 3**.
   h) If necessary, place the insertion point at the end of the "World's Leading Producers of Olives" heading.
   i) Press **Enter**.
   j) In the **Files** panel, select the **producers.txt** file and right-click it.

Note: To open a file from the **Files** panel, you can double-click it or right-click it and select **Open** from the pop-up menu.

k) Select **Open** from the pop-up menu.
l) Select all of the text.
m) On the **Application** bar, select **Edit→Copy**.
n) Close the **producers.txt** file.
o) On the **Application** bar, select **Edit→Paste**.
p) Select the text beginning with "Spain" and ending with "Portugal."

q) In the **Properties** panel, be sure the **HTML** button is chosen and select the **Ordered List** icon.
r) Click outside the sidebar text to deselect the unordered list.
s) Save your work with the name *my_history.html* and close the file and the **history.html** file.

ACTIVITY 3-5
Creating a Definition List

Data Files

olive_oil.html

olive_oil.txt

Scenario

There is a lot of confusion about the different types of olive oil and how one should use them. Your site should clear up much of the confusion and you know a definition list is the perfect format to list the oils and explain what they are and when to use them. This should clear up the uncertainty. You will format the text on the olive oil page into a definition list.

1. Open the **olive_oil.html** file.
   a) In the **Files** panel, double-click the **olive_oil.html** page to open it.
   b) Place the insertion point after the heading "Types of Olive Oil" and press **Enter**.
   c) In the **Files** panel select the **olive_oil.txt** file and select **Open**.
   d) Select all of the text beginning with "Extra-Virgin Olive Oil" and ending with the text in the last paragraph "was processed incorrectly."
   e) On the **Application** bar, select **Edit→Copy**.
   f) Close the **olive_oil.txt** file.
   g) On the **Application** bar, select **Edit→Paste**.
   h) Save the page as *my_olive_oil.html*

2. Create the definition list.
   a) Place the insertion point before the E in "Extra-Virgin."
   b) Scroll down to the end of the section.
   c) Hold down **Shift** and click after the text "was processed incorrectly."
   d) All of the olive oil types and their definitions should be selected.
   e) In the **Application** bar, select **Insert→HTML→Text Objects→Definition List**.
   f) Click in the white space of the page to deselect the definition list text.
   g) Save and close **my_olive_oil.html** and **olive_oil.html**.

Horizontal Rule

The horizontal rule is a convenient component used to separate content dealing with different topics. You create it simply by placing the insertion point at the location you wish the rule to appear and insert it. You can modify the horizontal rule in the **Properties** panel. The width and height can be specified. The width is expressed in absolute dimensions by pixels or relative dimensions by percentage (%) of the page. It is aligned to the center of the page by default, but you can move it to the left or right of the page as well. You can apply shading to the horizontal rule by using the **Shading** check box in the **Properties** panel.

 Access the Checklist tile on your LogicalCHOICE course screen for reference information and job aids on How to Create a Horizontal Rule

Quotations

Quotations are used to emphasize thoughts and concepts. When you included them within a paragraph, the quotations are set off with quotation marks. If you want to give the quotation special attention on a web page, you will place the quotation in a block quotation. The quotation is separated from the paragraph and centered on the page, directing the reader's full attention to it.

 Access the Checklist tile on your LogicalCHOICE course screen for reference information and job aids on How to Create a Block Quotation

ACTIVITY 3-6
Creating a Horizontal Rule and Block Quotation

Data File

my_history.html

Scenario

The recorded past of olives and olive oil is a blend of history and myth. The sagas are fascinating and you want to include as many as you can so the site visitor can learn about them. You have created the page to include history, tales of faith, and mythical anecdotes. In organizing the history page, you know that historic fact should be kept separate from myths and other accounts.

You have also included a remarkable quotation on the history page and would like to set it off as a block quotation to attract attention to it. You know that the HTML tag language has that capability and you want to use Dreamweaver to quickly apply the tag to the quote.

1. Create horizontal rules.
   a) In the **Files** panel, double-click the **my_history.html** file to open it.
   b) Place the insertion point just after "leaders." in the last sentence in the "History" text.
   c) On the **Application** bar, select **Insert→HTML→Horizontal Rule**.
   d) Place the insertion point just after "ages." in the last sentence in the "Olives and Faith" text.
   e) On the **Application** bar, select **Insert→HTML→Horizontal Rule**.
   f) Save your work.

2. Create a block quote
   a) Select the quote in the last paragraph of the "Olives and Faith" section on the page beginning with "Eat the olive oil" and ending with "disease in it... ."
   b) In the **Document** toolbar, select the **Code** button.
   c) In the **Code** panel, on the left of the workspace, select the **Wrap Tag** icon.
   d) Type **bl** and note that the **<blockquote>** tag is selected.
   e) Press **Enter** twice and note that a **<blockquote>** tag has been place around the quotation.
   f) Press the **Design** button.
   g) Save your work and then close the file.

TOPIC D

Set Page Properties

You can set the basic characteristics of each page by using the **Page Properties** dialog box. It gives you access to five groups of attributes, including **Appearance**, **Links**, **Headings**, and the **Title**. With the many attributes in one place, you can address most of the styling and placement decisions necessary for completing a page.

Setting Page Properties

The properties that can be set are font properties, margins, background colors or images, link colors, text colors, heading sizes and colors, and the page title.

Setting Font Properties

Font families are chosen in the page properties. They are listed in groups of three or four fonts. The purpose of listing fonts in groups is that the font you specified for your page may not be present on the site visitor's computer. For that reason the font groups contain a Windows font, a Mac font, and at least one generic font. When your page is displayed on the viewer's monitor, the browser will attempt to find and use the first font listed in the group. If it cannot find that font, it will attempt to find the second font listed. That procedure will continue until the font is found or the computer substitutes a similar font. If a font substitution actually occurs, the alignment of elements on the page may be disturbed due to the variations in the substituted font.

It is for this reason that it is strongly suggested that fonts chosen for the body text of your pages be fonts that are present on all standard computers.

Setting Paragraph Properties

The basic paragraph properties you can control are the alignment, first line indent, line height and margin. The alignment is done in the **Properties** panel with the **CSS** button selected. The other properties must be controlled by applying the styles to one or more paragraphs.

 Access the Checklist tile on your LogicalCHOICE course screen for reference information and job aids on **How to Set Page Properties**

ACTIVITY 3-7
Setting Font and Paragraph Properties

Data File

index.html

Scenario

You would like to save time in setting the final font and paragraph properties by setting them in a central location for each page. You also want to be sure that each page has a title for the search engines and the browser tabs. The one place where all of that is accomplished is in the **Page Properties** dialog box.

1. View page font choices and set the final font for the home page text.
   a) From the **Files** pane, open the **index.html** page.
   b) On the **Application** bar, select **Modify→Page Properties**.
   c) In the **Page Properties** dialog box, in the **Category** list, be sure the **Appearance (CSS)** category is chosen.
   d) Note that the **Page font** is currently set at **Verdana, Arial, Helvetica, sans-serif**.
   e) Examine the font's look and readability.
   f) Select the **Page font** drop-down arrow and select another font group.
   g) Select the **Apply** button.
   h) Assess the look and readability of the page text.
   i) Select other font groups and check their readability by choosing the **Apply** button.
   j) Select the **Page font** drop-down arrow again and select **Verdana, Geneva, sans-serif**.
   k) Select the **Apply** button.

2. Select standard colors for the headings.
   a) In the **Page Properties** dialog box, in the **Category** list, select the **Headings (CSS)** category.
   b) In the **Heading 1** row, place the insertion point in the text box after the **color swatch** square.
   c) Type **#4C6229** and press **Tab** three times to move to the **Heading 2** color text box.
   d) Type the same color in the **Heading 2** and **Heading 3** color text boxes.
   e) Select **OK**.
   f) Save the file.

3. Check the page in a browser.
   a) In the **Document** toolbar select the **Preview/Debug in browser** icon.
   b) Select **Preview in IExplore**.
   c) Note the appearance and location of the page elements.
   d) Close the browser and select **File→Close All** pages.

Summary

In this lesson, you created pages by using existing text. You added content for both the site visitor and the search engines. You now know the three types of lists used to display information, and that the headings and body text fonts are set in a central location.

What are some of the considerations you may want to keep in mind when adding meta tags to your site?

Do you think it's more important to have a banner that is eye-catching, or one that closely reflects the content of the website?

 Note: Check your LogicalCHOICE Course screen for opportunities to interact with your classmates, peers, and the larger LogicalCHOICE online community about the topics covered in this course or other topics you are interested in. From the Course screen you can also access available resources for a more continuous learning experience.

4 | Using CSS

Lesson Time: 30 minutes

Lesson Objectives

In this lesson, you will:

- Create styles and selectors with Cascading Style Sheets (CSS).

- Use CSS to format a web page.

Lesson Introduction

Cascading Style Sheets (CSS) is an extensive styling system that allows the web practitioner to control and style every element on the web page. It was created to separate content from formatting and style. With CSS, you can position, size, color, decorate, and cause to appear and disappear any component on a page.

TOPIC A

Create Styles and Selectors with CSS

Creating styles and selectors for CSS are the fundamental tools of styling and control exercised on page elements. The selectors identify the elements of the page to which the styles are applied. The browser merely reads the selectors, locates those elements, and applies the styles.

Advantages of CSS

The advantages of CSS are numerous. With CSS, the styling of content is made more consistent, is faster to apply, and is more easily maintained. Styles are read once by the browser and applied wherever directed. Search engines need not read the styles—they need only to read the content. Using CSS reduces page content and the pages download more quickly. Finally, CSS provides a far superior range of styling choices than HTML ever did. Another major advantage in using CSS styling is content reuse. Content used on web pages can, using alternate CSS styling, be prepared for print and audio products as well. Such versatility raises the CSS system of styling to the most cost effective, most desirable technique available.

CSS Rules for Formatting and Layout

Formatting styles consist of a styling statement, a colon, and a value followed by a semi-colon. You can apply as many styles as required for an element. The styles are listed between curly braces { }. The browser applies all of the styles listed to the element to which it is directed by the selector.

Example:
```
p { font-family: Verdana, Geneva, sans-serif;
    font-size: 12px;
    text-align: left;
    color: #000; }
```

Figure 4–1: A Typical Style Using a Tag Selector

Style statements are available for formatting text, images, component location, visibility, layering, and colors.

HTML Tag Selectors

Because every web page is made up of *HTML tags*, you will select HTML tag selectors to direct styles to those elements on the page. In many cases, HTML tags are nested within other HTML tags, and selectors will indicate a nested relationship. For example, an unordered list <ul> will have list items <li> nested within. Those list items may have anchor tags within them creating links of the text between the link item tags.

To direct a style or styles to the text forming the links, the selector required is **ul li a**. That is, the browser will apply the style to (reading right to left) the anchor tag <a> within the list item <li>, which is in the unordered list <ul>.

Class Name Selectors

When you want to apply a style to more than one element on the page, you will create a *class name*. It is generally used to identify more than one component on the page. The names you use should be descriptive and short. A typical use of a class name is to identify some, but not all, of the paragraphs on a page so you can direct special styling to those paragraphs but not others. Class names are shown in style notation with a leading period (.), for example: .sidebar.

ID Selectors

ID selectors are similar to class name selectors with one major difference: The ID is used to identify a single component on the page. No other element can use that selector name. IDs are generally used for unique elements such as divs. IDs are shown in style notation with a leading pound sign or hash mark (#), for example: #content.

Typical CSS Style Rules

A CSS style requires two components: a selector and one or more styles. The selector determines the page component to which the style is applied. The styles identify the characteristic of the content to be changed and how it should be changed. In CSS, you can create simple styles or complex styles. The page element itself determines what style is applied. The complexity of the style can be in its selector or in the number of style rules used.

Some typical styles are included in the following table.

Style	Effect of the Selector	Effect of the Style	Type of Style
h1{ font-family: Arial, Helvetica, sans-serif; **font-size**: 18 px; **color**: #4C6229; **}**	Style is applied to all HTML **Heading 1**	Arial, 18 pixels, olive green color	Directed to a simple HTML tag
.nav a { font-style: italic; **font-weight**: bold; **text-align**: center; **}**	Style is applied only to **anchor tags** in a component with the **class name .nav**	Bold, italic, centered	Directed to a compound HTML tag
. side space { background-color: #FFF; **margin-left**: 25px; **margin-top**: 10px; **line height**: 110%; **}**	All components on the page with the **class name .sidespace**	Background color white, 25 pixel margin on the left and 10 pixels on top, text line height increased by 10%	Directed to a simple class name
# footer p { font-style: italic; **border-bottom**: 3px solid #90EE90; **}**	All paragraphs in the component with the singular **ID** of **footer**	Font is italic with a bottom border that is 3 pixels wide, solid, and colored light green	Directed only to the paragraphs in the component with the ID

The Cascade in CSS

CSS styles may be placed in three different locations on a page. How they interact is the definition of the cascade. The cascade allows all three locations to work together with the browser selecting the most specific styling for a component even if conflicts are present.

A style may be directed to an element by placing it inline or inside its HTML tag: <p style="color: #0000FF">. This style was inserted into the paragraph tag. More typically, styles are placed between <style> tags in the <head> section of the page. These styles are typically referred to as internal style sheet or an *embedded style sheet*. Embedded styles apply only to the page on which they are placed. The third location for CSS styles is in an external style sheet. The advantage of an external style sheet is it can be linked to multiple pages obviating the necessity of repeating styles on every page. Also, if styles are modified, they need only be modified in one location for the changes to be applied to multiple pages. Multiple external style sheets can be linked to multiple pages. On many sites all three locations (inline, internal, and external style sheets) are used for placing styles.

If there are conflicting styles on the various style sheets, the browser chooses the most specific style, which is usually the inline style, if present.

Note: For more information about how to use an embedded style to make an external style sheet, check out the LearnTO **Create an External Style Sheet from an Embedded Style** presentation by clicking the **LearnTO** tile on your LogicalCHOICE Course screen.

Access the Checklist tile on your LogicalCHOICE course screen for reference information and job aids on How to Create a Style and Selector

ACTIVITY 4–1
Creating Styles and Selectors

Data File

harvest.html

Scenario

The harvest.html page is nearly done, but it has several elements that need to be styled. The marketing manager has asked to see the page so you need to get it done quickly. You will add color to the sidebar and the navigation buttons.

1. Name a new site for this lesson.
   a) Select **Site→New Site**.
   b) In the **Site Setup for Unnamed Site** dialog box, in the **Site Name** text box, type the site name *4EE*

2. Identify the site root folder.
   a) To the right of the **Local Site Folder** text box, select the **Browse for folder** 📁 icon.
   b) In the **Choose Root Folder** dialog box, navigate to the **C:\092001Data\Using CSS** folder.
   c) Select **Open** and then **Select**.

3. Identify the **graphics** folder.
   a) In the **Site Setup for 4EE** dialog box, select **Advanced Settings**.
   b) To the right of the **Default Images folder** text box, select the **Browse for folder** 📁 icon.
   c) Select the **graphics** folder.
   d) Select **Open**.
   e) Select **Select**.

4. Save the site and confirm the listing of the site folders.
   a) Select the **Save** button.
   b) In the **Files** panel, note the site root folder **Using CSS** and the **graphics** folder.

5. Change the sidebar background and text color.
   a) In the **Files** panel, double-click the **harvest.html** page to open it.
   b) Place the insertion point in the sidebar area.
   c) In the **CSS Styles** panel, select the **All** button.
   d) In the **All Rules** section, select the **.sidebar1** selector and rule.
   e) Under **Properties for ".sidebar1"** select the existing **background-color #FFF**.
   f) Type *#471803* and press **Enter**.
   g) Scroll down and select the **color** property.
   h) Type *#C3D003* and press **Enter**.
   i) Save the file as *my_harvest.html*

6. Change the background color and text color of the navigation buttons.
   a) Place the insertion point in one of the navigation buttons (**Link one**) in the sidebar.
   b) In the **CSS Styles** panel, select the **Current** button.
   c) Under **Rules**, select the **ul.nav a, ul.nav a:visited <a>** rule.

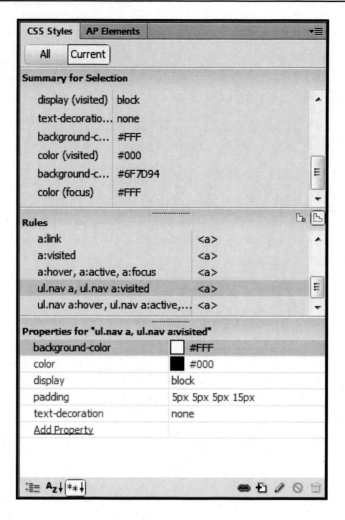

d) Under **Properties for "ul.nav a, ul.nav a:visited <a>"** select the existing **background-color #FFF**.

e) Type *#ABC405* and press **Enter**.

f) Select the existing **color** (text color) **#000**, type *#471803* and press **Enter**.

g) Select the **Add Property** link.

h) Type the letter *F* and select the drop-down arrow.

i) Scroll down to the property **font-weight** and select it.

j) From the drop-down list next to **font-weight**, select **bold**.

7. Preserve the color of the ordered list heading in the sidebar.

a) In the sidebar, select the heading "World's Leading Producers of Olives."

b) At the bottom of the **CSS Styles** panel, select the **New CSS Rule** ⬚ icon.

c) If necessary, under **Selector Type,** select the **Compound (based on your selection)** option. and select **OK**.

d) In the **CSS Rule definition for .container .sidebar1 h3** dialog box, in the **Category Type** in the **Color** text box, type *#C3D003* and press **Enter**.

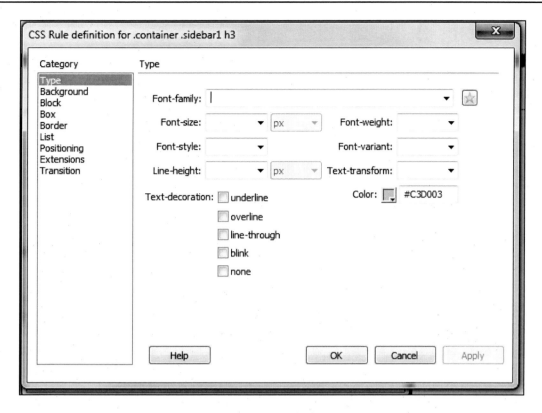

e) Close the **harvest.html** file. Save the **my_harvest.html** file and leave it open for the next activity.

TOPIC B

Use CSS to Format a Web Page

The styles you will likely apply to a page are margins and padding, which are used to keep components separated and located appropriately. Both margins and padding are applied similarly. When considering margins and padding, you should understand the CSS Box.

The CSS Box

Every element you use on a page (text, list, graphic, or table) is considered to be in a virtual box. You may add padding around the box on one, two, three, or all four sides, keeping the content spaced away from a border if you choose to use one. Additionally, you may add a margin outside the border on one or more sides, keeping the content, padding, and border away from other elements on the page.

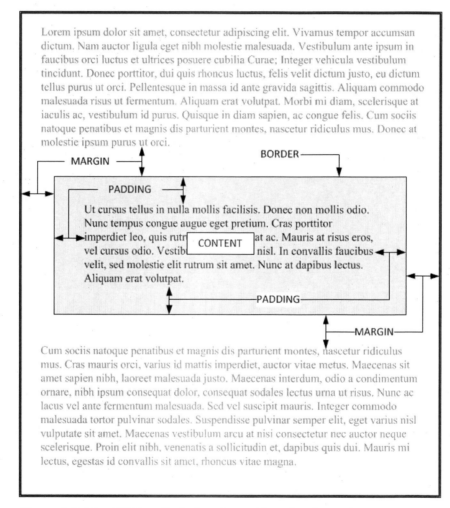

Figure 4-2: The CSS Box displaying the padding, border and margins.

CSS Rules

Margin styles include margin-top, margin-right, margin-bottom, and margin-left, as do padding styles. Each can be set to different values such as in the following style for a paragraph:

```
p { margin-top: 10px
    margin-right: 15px;
    margin-bottom: 12px;
    margin-left: 13px; }
```

In Dreamweaver, the simplest method to set margins for the page is to select **Modify→Page Properties** from the **Application** bar. Padding and margins for components on the page are created in the CSS Styles panel. Construct the style by using a selector directing the style to the component desired.

ACTIVITY 4-2
Formatting a Page Using CSS

Data File

copyright.txt

background.png

Before You Begin

my_harvest.html is open.

Scenario

Continuing the completion of the harvest page, you will adjust the position of some elements, change several colors, and add footer content.

---

1. Change the main heading color and extend sidebar color.
   a) On the **Application** bar, select **Modify→Page Properties**.
   b) In the **Page Properties** dialog box, select the **Headings (CSS)** category.
   c) In the **Heading 1 color** text box (last text box after the color swatch), type *#4C6229* and press **Enter**.
   d) In the sidebar, place the insertion point after the word "Portugal.".
   e) Hold down **Shift** and press **Enter** as many times as it takes to extend the background color to the footer.

2. Relocate the ordered list within the sidebar.
   a) Place the insertion point just before the word "Spain" in the sidebar.
   b) At the bottom of the **CSS Styles** panel, select the **New CSS Rule** icon.
   c) Confirm that in the **New CSS Rule** dialog box, the selector name is **.container .sidebar1 ol li**.
   d) Select **OK**.
   e) In the **CSS Rule definition for .container .sidebar1 ol li**, select the **Category Box**.
   f) In the **Margin** section, uncheck **Same for all**.
   g) In the **Left margin** text box, type *75* and be sure **px** is selected in the units drop-down menu.
   h) Select **Apply** and inspect the new location of the ordered list.
   i) Select **OK**.
   j) Save your work.

3. Format and add content to the footer.
   a) Delete any text that is in the footer.
   b) Open the copyright text file **copyright.txt**.
   c) Select all of the text. Copy it and close the **copyright.txt** file.
   d) Paste the text in the footer.
   e) In the **CSS Styles** panel, select the **All** button.
   f) Under **Rules**, select the **.footer** selector and rule.
   g) Select the **background-color** text and type *#ABC045*
   h) Select **Add Property**, type the letter *C* and scroll to and select the **color-profile** property.
   i) In the text box to the right, type *#471803* and press **Enter**.

4. Format the page background for higher resolution monitors. If gray or white areas appear outside the formatted page, it indicates that the computer monitor is one that has a horizontal resolution higher than 1,075 pixels. If that condition exists, do the following:

    a) In the **CSS Styles** panel, under **All Rules**, select the **body** selector and rule.

    b) Under **Properties for "body"** select **Add Property**.

    c) Type *B* and select the **background-image** property from the list.

    d) To the right of the **background-image** property select the **folder** icon.

    e) Open the **graphics** folder and select **background.png** and select **OK**.

    f) The background area is filled with a gradient created in Photoshop.

    g) Save your work and preview the page in the browser.

    h) Close **my_harvest.html**.

Summary

In this lesson, you explored the styling capability of the Cascading Style Sheets (CSS) system. CSS styles help control color, positioning, text formatting, and other page attributes.

What CSS style would you choose to move page elements away from the current paragraph on which you are working?

Can you think of a reason a website developer would not want to use one single external style sheet to style an entire website?

 Note: Check your LogicalCHOICE Course screen for opportunities to interact with your classmates, peers, and the larger LogicalCHOICE online community about the topics covered in this course or other topics you are interested in. From the Course screen you can also access available resources for a more continuous learning experience.

5 | Inserting Images

Lesson Time: 45 minutes

Lesson Objectives

In this lesson, you will:

- Insert images.
- Manage image properties with CSS.

Lesson Introduction

Images supply more than half of the interest in websites. They add color and information to sites that cannot be accomplished efficiently in any other way. The graphics should add detail and intelligence that is relevant to the content of the page.

TOPIC A

Insert Images

Adding graphics to web pages requires two basic skills—the ability to determine what kind of graphic is best to use and the ability to choose an appropriate location on the page. Graphics that are colorful and have a basic focal point are best. Size is another important characteristic. The graphic should be large enough to easily discern its content but not so large that it extends the time for the graphic to be downloaded from the server while the site visitor waits.

Graphic File Formats

There are only three graphic formats that can be used in web pages: Graphic Interchange Format (.gif), Joint Photographic Experts Group (.jpg or .jpeg), and Portable Network Graphics (.png). They each have unique characteristics that are suitable for use on the Web.

Graphic	Color Capacity	Supports Transparency	Generally Used For
GIF	256	Yes, single color	Illustrations, logos, clip art, cartoons, drawings, animations
JPG or JPEG	16.7 million	No	Photographs (loses some detail when compressed)
PNG	16.7 million	Yes	Photographs, illustrations, logos, clip art, cartoons, and drawings (no loss during compression but results in larger files)

Images from Other Adobe Applications

Images and graphics can be created, processed, and optimized in other Adobe products such as Photoshop, Illustrator, Flash, and Fireworks. Adobe Bridge is also helpful as a repository and data store for graphic files. The most popular tool for creating and processing graphics for the Web is Photoshop, which can save files in all three graphic types. Images can be optimized for the Web in both Photoshop and Fireworks. These images, if to be used in a web page, should be saved within the local root folder.

Requirement of Saving Image Files in the Local Root Folder

A graphics or images folder should be created within the root folder to hold all supporting graphics. When graphics are inserted into the pages, they will automatically get stored in the graphics folder. This is primarily because Dreamweaver will store the page files in the site root folder and maintains the link connections, whenever new pages are designed and linked to other destinations.

The Image Alternate Text and Title Attributes

Graphics cannot be "read" by the search engines. On their own, graphics cannot contribute useful information to direct visitors to the site. However, the alternate text and title attributes provides an opportunity to add textual data to the page that search engines can read, collect, store, and use to identify your site to searchers.

Section 508 of the Rehabilitation Act of 1973, amended in 1992 and 1998 to include access to electronic and information technology, recommends that websites be accessible to persons with physical challenges. Although the recommendations apply to the entirety of websites, they particularly relate to the placement of graphics. The alternate text added to graphic attributes not only provides content for the search engine, but also provides data for screen-reading technology to voice for sight-impaired website visitors. Additionally, the title attribute is displayed whenever the mouse pointer hovers over a graphic, and then that graphic's title is spoken aloud by the screen reader.

 Access the Checklist tile on your LogicalCHOICE course screen for reference information and job aids on How to Insert Images

ACTIVITY 5–1
Inserting an Image on a Page

Data Files

index.html

harvest.html

olives_leaves.jpg

harvest_tool.jpg

Scenario

You have received compliments on the pages you constructed but everyone is asking whether you will use photos or graphics to perk up the site. The marketing manager has hinted that she has particular expectations as to what photos should be used. You plan to meet with her and get her suggestions.

1. Create a new site for this lesson.
   a) Select **Site→New Site**.
   b) In the **Site Setup for Unnamed Site** dialog box, in the **Site Name** text box, type the site name, *5EE*

2. Identify the site root folder.

   a) To the right of the **Local Site Folder** text box, select the **Browse for folder** 🗀 icon.
   b) In the **Choose Root Folder** dialog box, navigate to the **C:\092001Data\Inserting Images** folder.
   c) Select the **Open** button and select the **Select** button.

3. Identify the **graphics** folder.
   a) In the **Site Setup for 5EE** dialog box, select **Advanced Settings**.

   b) To the right of the **Default Images folder** text box, select the **Browse for folder** 🗀 icon.
   c) Select the **graphics** folder.
   d) Select the **Open** button.
   e) Select the **Select** button.

4. Save the site and confirm the listing of the site folders.
   a) Select the **Save** button.
   b) In the **Files** panel, note the site root folder, **Inserting Images**, and the **graphics** folder.

5. Place an image on the page, enter the alternate text, and add a title attribute for the graphic.
   a) Open **index.html**.
   b) Place the insertion point before the first word of the first paragraph that says "The olive has… ."
   c) On the **Application** bar, select **Insert→Image**.
   d) Open the **graphics** folder, select **olives_leaves.jpg**, and select **OK**.
   e) In the **Image Tag Accessibility Attributes** dialog box, in the **Alternate text** text box, type *Ripe Olives with Leaves* and select **OK**.
   f) If necessary, select the graphic, and then select the **Code** button.
   g) Place the insertion point after the closing quotes of the **alt** attribute.

```
alt="Ripe Olives with Leaves" />The olive has a long
iod of its life. We, as human beings, are the
e olive tree does not reach a bountiful harvest until
```

h) Press the **Spacebar** and type *title="Ripe Olives with Leaves"*
i) In the **CSS Styles** panel, select the **Refresh** button and select the **Design** button.
j) Save the page and preview it in the browser.
k) Move the mouse pointer over the graphic. The graphic title will appear.
l) Close the browser.

6. Place a graphic within text on the page.
   a) Open **harvest.html**.
   b) Place the insertion point before the first word of the second paragraph "Harvesting can be done... ."
   c) On the **Application** bar, select **Insert→Image**.
   d) If necessary, open the **graphics** folder, select **harvest_tool.jpg**, and select **OK**.
   e) In the **Image Tag Accessibility Attributes** dialog box, in the **Alternate text** text box, type *Harvesting Olives with a Hand Tool* and select **OK**.
   f) Select the graphic and select the **Code** button.
   g) Place the insertion point after the closing quotes of the **alt** attribute.
   h) Press the **Spacebar** and type *title="Harvesting Olives with a Hand Tool"*
   i) In the **CSS Styles** panel, select the **Refresh** button and then the **Design** button.
   j) Save the page as *my_harvest.html* and preview it in the browser.
   k) Move the mouse pointer over the graphic. The graphic title will appear.
   l) Close the browser and all files.

TOPIC B

Manage Image Properties with CSS

A web page's graphic images can be formatted for size, position, and border. Although graphic adjustments can be accomplished in Dreamweaver, it is recommended that all sizing, optimizing, and color adjusting be made in a photo-editing product more suited to that purpose. Graphics are also candidates for linking to other pages. CSS styles are the tools used to move and border graphics to desired locations. Small adjustments to size are made by using the HTML image <img> tag attributes in the **Properties** panel.

Alignment Properties

Images, when placed on the page, can be floated left or right with the CSS style float. This allows any text that is vying for the same space to wrap around the photo. If the float style is not used, the graphic will sit on the text baseline as if it were an oversized character. Margins and padding are used to control the separation of the image from other elements, such as text and borders.

CSS Image Properties

The image properties controllable with HTML attributes in the **Properties** panel are height and width, cropping, brightness and contrast, and sharpening. Recognizing that most of these attributes are best adjusted in Photoshop, Dreamweaver has an icon in the **Properties** panel that switches to Photoshop and loads the selected graphic for editing.

CSS styles provide for floating images on the page, allowing text to wrap around the graphic. The styles selection includes choices to repeat background images for pattern effects, shadowing graphics, sizing them, and placing surrounding borders.

Inserting and Controlling Images

Images are inserted in web pages in the position where the graphic is nearest the associated text information. Then the image is sized, if necessary, and it is positioned by floating it right or left. Borders are applied with the CSS border style at any time.

The Need for Images to be kept at Original Size

When you want to modify the size of an image in a web page after its insertion, do not try to resize or scale the image in Design view. If you do so, then the image may not be displayed properly in the browser. Chances are that the image may appear skewed and distorted. Try to retain the image in its original size or use an external image-editing application to scale or resize images. To ensure that the images are displayed properly, you can also set the width and height that correspond to the actual width and height of the image in the **Properties** panel, and Dreamweaver will automatically update the values that you specify with the image's original dimensions.

 Access the Checklist tile on your LogicalCHOICE course screen for reference information and job aids on How to Manage Image Properties with CSS

ACTIVITY 5-2
Inserting Additional Images and CSS Controls

Data Files

olive_oil.html

flavored.jpg

my_harvest.html

index.html

Scenario

Your colleagues at Emerald Epicure are curious about the website, constantly dropping by to see it as it develops. On their last visit they were wondering why you inserted graphics on the pages and left them sitting at the left of the page. They also mentioned that they looked odd sitting on the same line with the text. You explained that you intend to move them and have the text wrap around the photos. They can't wait to see you do that. You've invited them for a viewing after you're done.

1. Place a graphic and wrap the text around it.
   a) Open **olive_oil.html**.
   b) Place the insertion point before the first word of the first paragraph.
   c) On the **Application** bar, select **Insert→Image**.
   d) If necessary, open the **graphics** folder, then select **flavored.jpg**, and select **OK**.
   e) In the **Image Tag Accessibility Attributes** dialog box, in the **Alternate text** text box, type *Flavored Olive Oil* and select **OK**.
   f) Be sure the graphic is selected.

    Note: To confirm that the graphic has been selected, look at the **Properties** panel and confirm that a thumbnail version of the graphic is displayed there.

   g) In the **CSS Styles** panel, select the **New Style** button.
   h) In the **New CSS Rule** dialog box, note that the selector chosen by Dreamweaver is the **.container .content p img**, which is a result of the image being selected.
   i) Select **OK**.
   j) In the **CSS Rule definition** dialog box, select the **Category Box**.
   k) Select the **Float** drop-down arrow, select **right** and select **OK**.
   l) Save the file as *my_olive_oil.html* and preview it in the browser.

2. Position another graphic.
   a) Open **index.html**.
   b) Select the **olives with leaves** graphic.
   c) In the **CSS Styles** panel, select the **New Style** button.
   d) In the **New CSS Rule** dialog box, note that the selector chosen by Dreamweaver is the **.container .content p img**, which is a compound selector identifying this specific image only.
   e) Select **OK**.
   f) In the **CSS Rule definition** dialog box, select the **Category Box**.
   g) Select the **Float** drop-down arrow, select **left**, and select **OK**.
   h) Save the page and preview it in the browser.

3. Position a graphic within text.

    a) Open **my_harvest.html**.

    b) Select the **harvest** graphic.

    c) In the **CSS Styles** panel, select the **New Style** button.

    d) Select **OK**.

    e) In the **CSS Rule definition** dialog box, select the **Category Box**.

    f) Select the **Float** drop-down arrow, select **right**, and select **Apply**.

    g) In the **Padding** section, uncheck the **Same for all** check box.

    h) In the **Right** box, enter *25* and, in the **Left** box, enter *25*

    i) Select **Apply**.

    j) Adjust the padding dimensions to suit. Select **OK** when you are done.

    k) Save the page and preview it in the browser.

    l) Close all open files.

Summary

In this lesson, you added graphics to the web pages to heighten interest in the subject. Using CSS to place objects and move them to better locations allows text to wrap around the graphics, enhancing their correlation.

When might you consider using JPG image files in a website over PNG image files? Vice versa?

What are some benefits of using alternate applications, such as Adobe® Photoshop®, to develop the images for your website?

Note: Check your LogicalCHOICE Course screen for opportunities to interact with your classmates, peers, and the larger LogicalCHOICE online community about the topics covered in this course or other topics you are interested in. From the Course screen you can also access available resources for a more continuous learning experience.

6 | Inserting Tables and Importing Content

Lesson Time: 1 hour

Lesson Objectives

In this lesson, you will:

- Construct a table of products by using table tags and properties.

- Import external data.

Lesson Introduction

Tables are important tools for web pages because they provide structure and display information in an orderly fashion. Although CSS <div> tags supplant tables for organizing pages, tables still have a useful purpose in displaying large quantities of data.

Importing content from other sources requires some processing in order to remove artifacts present in the original application that can contribute to unintended formatting.

TOPIC A

Table Tags and Properties

Tables require many tags to be constructed properly. There are tags for the table itself and tags for rows, headers, cells, and captions. However, tables are easily constructed and modified in Dreamweaver. You will focus on the number of rows and columns required and how to style the various elements with CSS.

Typical Use of Tables

In a web page, tables are used for two purposes: laying out a page to provide areas for headings, text content, and graphics; and displaying large amounts of complicated data. Because the visible presence of the table can be hidden, it was a perfect but rigid tool for creating page layouts. CSS has changed this, and most practitioners prefer CSS <div> tags for laying out a page. As for using tables in a web page to display data, it's not likely that tables be superseded by CSS.

Advantages of Div Containers vs. Table Cell Layout

Div containers or table cells help in defining a logical division of the content within a web page. A layout drawn using either of them has its own advantages.

- When a layout is drawn using the Div containers, control is established over the space utilized by the content. The containers expand or contract depending on the volume of text or size of the image that is added to the container. The physical properties and attributes of every Div container can be varied depending on what's needed.
- When a layout is drawn using table, it provides dedicated areas for headings, text, and images. Tables are also useful when a large amount of complex data is to be displayed in a page. Tables are useful when data of similar category is to be shown.

Table Cell Contents

Once the rows and columns of a table are determined and placed on the page, the cells of the table can be used for almost any purpose. You can place text, graphics, and even another table in a cell. This handy use of the cell space gives you freedom to use the table for whatever purpose you can imagine. Table cells are sometimes colored or have a background graphic placed.

Nested Tables

When the contents of a table cell will be too complex to manage, another table is inserted in that cell to organize the data and information. Called a *nested table*, this is a simple solution for laying out data and information in an organized fashion, making it easy to understand for the site visitor.

Table Tags and Attributes

Table construction on a web page requires multiple tags.

Table Tag s	Purpose	Attributes
<table>	Defines the table	border, cellpadding, cellspacing, summary, width
<tr>	Defines row elements	align, valign

Table Tag s	Purpose	Attributes
\<th>	Denotes a table header	align, colspan, rowspan, valign
\<td>	Denotes a standard cell	align, colspan, rowspan, valign

The Table Dialog Box

The table dialog box gives the page producer a choice of most of the attributes of the table, including the number of rows and columns, column headers, row headers or both, border thickness, cell padding and spacing, caption, and summary.

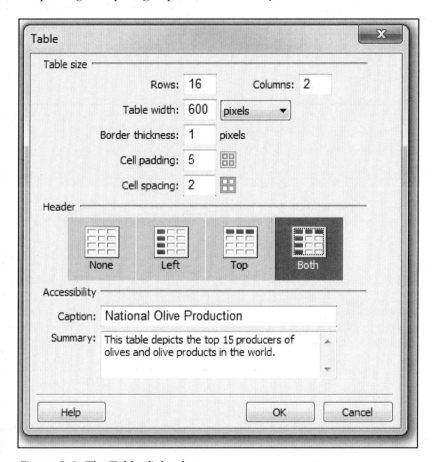

Figure 6-1: The Table dialog box.

The Table Widths Visual Aid

When constructing the page, you might find it helpful to see the table and column widths. These attributes are easily turned on and off as required by selecting the **Visual Aids** icon in the **Document** toolbar and selecting **Table Widths**. If a clearer view of the table is required, the widths can be turned off.

Controlling Table Width and Alignment

With the table-selected column widths, table width and row heights can be adjusted by using the mouse. Some users prefer changing these dimensions numerically. Numerical adjustments of table dimensions are done in the **Properties** panel.

CSS Styling and Layout Rules for Tables

Numerous CSS styles apply to tables and table components. Styling is commonly applied to table borders, table width and height, text alignment, padding, font color, cell and table background colors, table caption position, and alternate row background color.

 Note: For more information about formatting tables, check out the LearnTO **Format Alternate Rows of a Table** presentation by clicking the **LearnTO** tile on your LogicalCHOICE Course screen.

Selecting Table Elements

Because table elements are nested within each other, selecting a particular cell or row is sometimes difficult. The simplest way to select a table element is to use the **Tag Selector**. By placing the insertion point in the table or in a specific cell of the table, you can select that cell, its row, or the entire table by choosing the appropriate tag in the **Tag Selector**.

 Access the Checklist tile on your LogicalCHOICE course screen for reference information and job aids on **How to Create a Table**

ACTIVITY 6-1
Creating a Table

Data File

products.html

Scenario

The president of Emerald Epicure Ltd. has been looking over the pages you have constructed and is pleased with the results. However, he is getting impatient. He asked when the products page would be complete because he wants to get it online before the competitors have a chance to revise their sites. You have the page started but you need to add the products with their photos. You promise him it will be done shortly.

1. Create a new site for this lesson.
   a) Select **Site→ New Site**.
   b) In the **Site Setup for Unnamed Site** dialog box, in the **Site Name** text box, type the site name, *6EE*

2. Identify the site root folder.
   a) To the right of the **Local Site Folder** text box, select the **Browse for folder** 🗀 icon.
   b) In the **Choose Root Folder** dialog box, navigate to the **C:\092001Data\Inserting Tables and Importing Content** folder.
   c) Select the **Open** button and then the **Select** button.

3. Create and identify the **graphics** folder.
   a) In the **Site Setup for 6EE** dialog box, select **Advanced Settings**.
   b) To the right of the **Default Images folder** text box, select the **Browse for folder** 🗀 icon.
   c) Select the **graphics** folder.
   d) Select the **Open** button.
   e) Select the **Select** button.

4. Save the site and confirm the listing of the site folders.
   a) Select the **Save** button.
   b) In the **Files** panel, note the site root folder, **Inserting Tables and Importing Content**, and the **graphics** folder.

5. Add a table to a page.
   a) Open the **products.html** file.
   b) Place the insertion point at the end of the last paragraph, before the footer, and press **Enter**.
   c) On the **Application** bar, select **Insert→Table**.
   d) In the **Table** dialog box, in the **Rows** box, type *4* and, in the **Columns** box, type *3*
   e) In the **Table width** box, type *900* and ensure that the drop-down option is **pixels**.
   f) Type *1* in the **Border thickness** box, type *15* in the **Cell padding** box, and type *2* in the **Cell spacing** box.
   g) In the **Header** section, select the **Both** header choice.
   h) Select **OK**.

6. Add product titles to the table.

a) In the second row, in the first column, type *Olive Oils*

 Note: In Dreamweaver, when the first entry is made into a new table, the column widths may change. They will continue to adjust as other content is entered into the remaining cells. As in other applications, the cell borders can be moved with the mouse pointer for final adjustment.

b) In the third row, in the first column, type *Olive Pastes and Tapenades*
c) In the fourth row, in the first column, type *Cured Olives*
d) Place the insertion point in the first row.
e) In the **Tag Selector**, select the **<tr>** tag.
f) In the **Properties** panel, select the **Merge selected cells using spans** [icon] button.
g) Click in the first row and type *Olive-Based Products*

 Note: The table widths are useful for creating tables with specific dimensions. They can be removed when no longer needed.

h) If the table widths are not shown above the table, in the **Document** toolbar, select the **Visual Aids** [icon] icon and select **Table Widths**.
i) Note the table and column widths shown above the table.
j) Save your work as *my_products.html* and leave the file open for the next activity. Close **products.html**.

ACTIVITY 6-2
Formatting a Table

Data Files

tapenade.jpg

cured.jpg

olive_oil.jpg

Before You Begin

The file my_products.html is open.

Scenario

You have begun to add products to the products page but to complete the page you need to add the graphical content, and format the table.

---

1. Add graphics to the table.

    a) Move the mouse pointer to the column divider between the first and second columns of the table.

    b) When the mouse pointer changes to a double vertical line and double arrow cursor, click and hold the left mouse button and move the column divider to the left, making the first column about 2 inches in width.

    c) Do the same for the column divider between the second and third columns, leaving the second column about 1 1/2 inches in width.

    d) Place the insertion point in the second row, second column.

    e) On the **Application** bar, select **Insert→Image**.

    f) In the **graphics** folder, select the **olive_oil.jpg** file and select **OK**.

    g) In the **Image Tag Accessibility Attributes** dialog box, in the **Alternative text** text box, type *Olive Oil* and select **OK**.

    h) For the next two rows do the same as steps 1d to 1g, using the following information:

Row	Graphic	Alternate Text
3	**tapenade.jpg**	*Olive Tapenade*
4	**cured.jpg**	*Cured Olives*

2. Center the table on the page.

    a) Click in any cell of the table.

    b) In the **Tag Selector**, select the **\<table\>** tag.

    c) In the **Properties** panel, select the **Align** drop-down arrow and select **Center**.

3. Remove the table widths.

    a) In the **Document** toolbar, select the **Visual Aids** 📷 icon.

    b) Select **Table Widths** to uncheck it.

4. Format the table header text.

    a) Select the header "Olive-Based Products" in the first row of the table.

    b) In the **CSS Styles** panel select **Current**.

    c) In the **Properties for ".container .content table tr th"**, ensure that the value for **color** is **#4C6229**.

---

d) In the **Properties** panel, be sure the **HTML** button is selected.

e) From the **Format** drop-down list, select **Heading 3**.

f) Save the file and leave it open for the next activity.

TOPIC B

Import External Data

All information used on web pages need not be originally prepared information. Any digitally available material can be used by importing it into Dreamweaver. This includes textual data as well as spreadsheet data. Imported data is accepted from a variety of sources.

The Import Commands

The **Import** command is in the **File** menu and provides a choice of **XML** files, **Word** files, **Excel** files, and **Tabular** files. Some files may have to be preprocessed to clean up artifacts that are contained in such files.

Word HTML Files

If the file you wish to import is a web page (.html) created in Microsoft® Word, it should be cleaned up because it may have superfluous internal tags and space allocations that are not required for a web page. Dreamweaver's **Clean Up Word HTML** command was created specifically to clean Word HTML files of these extra tags.

 Access the Checklist tile on your LogicalCHOICE course screen for reference information and job aids on How to Import External Data

ACTIVITY 6-3
Importing Data from Word Documents

Data File
olive_product_data.docx

Before You Begin
The file my_products.html is open.

Scenario
Your colleague has helped you save time by preparing a Word document that contains descriptions of the various products you included on the Products.html page. You will import it into Dreamweaver, and create a class name and style to format it.

1. Insert the content of a Word document into your page.
    a) Place the insertion point in the second row, third column.
    b) On the **Application** bar, select **File→Import→Word Document**.
    c) In the **Import Word Document** dialog box, from the **Inserting Tables and Importing Content** folder, select **olive_product_data.docx**.
    d) Select the **Open** button.
    e) In the table, in the second row, third column, scroll to the bottom of the text and select the text beginning with "Cured olives are" and ending with "fruit of the olive tree."
    f) Select **Edit→Cut**. Scroll down to the last row and click in the third column.
    g) Select **Edit→Paste**.
    h) In the second row, third column, scroll to the bottom of the text and select the text beginning with "Emerald Epicure's" and ending with "fish, fowl or meats."
    i) Select **Edit→Cut**. Scroll down to the third row and click in the third column.
    j) Select **Edit→Paste**.
    k) Click at the bottom of the cell in the second row, in the third column, below the olive oil text but above the cell boundary.
    l) Press **Backspace** twice to remove extra space left by the imported text.

2. Create a class name and CSS style for the product description text.
    a) Place the insertion point at the beginning of the text in the second row, third column.
    b) Select the **Code** button.
    c) Place the insertion point immediately after the **td**.

```
<td width="357"><p>Our olive oils
ers.  Both gourmets and health
ed in growing popularity for our oil
```

    d) Press the **Spacebar** and type *class="prod"*
    e) Select the **leading space** and **class="prod"** including the quotation marks.
    f) Copy the selection.
    g) Scroll down and locate the **<td>** tag before "Emerald Epicure."
    h) Place the insertion point immediately after the **td**.
    i) Paste at that location.
    j) Scroll down and locate the **<td>** tag before "Cured olives."

k) Place the insertion point immediately after the **td**.

l) Paste at that location.

m) Select the **Design** button.

n) Save your work.

3. Create a style for the prod class.

a) At the bottom of the **CSS Styles** panel, select the **New CSS Rule** icon.

b) In the **New CSS Rule** dialog box, be sure the **Selector Type** drop-down option is **Class (can apply to any HTML element)**.

c) In the **Selector Name** box, press the **period** key and type *prod.* The result should be **.prod**.

d) Select **OK**.

e) In the **CSS Rule definition** dialog box, select the **Block** category.

f) Select the **Text-align** drop-down arrow and select **left**.

g) Select **OK**.

h) Save your work and preview the page in the browser.

i) Close the browser and all files.

ACTIVITY 6–4
Importing Data from Excel

Data Files

world.html

world_stats_olives.xlsx

Scenario

The marketing manager maintains statistics from a leading authority about the world production and consumption of olive oil. She keeps the data in an Excel workbook and suggests that you include a page showing the data. You will prepare the page, import the Excel data, and format it to be consistent with the site.

1. Prepare a page for holding Excel data.
   a) Open **world.html**.
   b) Place the insertion point at the end of the last paragraph.
   c) Press **Enter**.
   d) Select **File→Import→Excel Document**.
   e) Select the **world_stats_olives.xlsx** file and select **Open**.

2. Format the data table.
   a) Place the insertion point in any cell of the table.
   b) In the **Tag Selector**, select the **<table>** tag.
   c) In the **Properties** panel, in the **Align** drop-down menu, select **Center**.
   d) Place the insertion point in the first row of the table.
   e) In the **Tag Selector**, select the **<tr>** tag.
   f) Select the **Merges selected cells using spans** [icon] button.
   g) Place the insertion point in the second row of the table.
   h) Select the **<tr>** tag and merge the cells.
   i) Select rows 1 and 2 by clicking and dragging from row 1 down to row 2.
   j) In the **Properties** panel, in the **Bg** color text box, type **#ABC045** and press **Enter**.
   k) If necessary, in the **Properties** panel, select the **HTML** button.
   l) Select the text "Global Market," and in the **Properties** panel select the **Bold** button.
   m) Click elsewhere in the text to deselect the title.

3. Add a border to the table.
   a) Place the insertion point in any cell of the table.
   b) From the **Tag Selector**, select **<table>**.
   c) In the **Properties** panel, in the **Border** text box, type **10**
   d) In the **CellPad** text box, type **3** and press **Enter**.
   e) Select the **New CSS Rule** icon.
   f) From the **Selector Type** drop-down list, select **Tag.**
   g) From the **Selector Name** drop-down list, be sure **table** is selected.
   h) Select **OK**.
   i) In **CSS Rule definition for table**, select the **Border** category.
   j) In the **Color** column, uncheck **Same for all**.
   k) In the **Top** and **Left** color boxes, type **#F1EA01**

l) In the **Right** and **Bottom** color boxes, type *#A0BD05*

m) Select **OK** and view the results.

n) Save the file as *my_world.html* and preview the page in the browser.

o) Close all open files.

Summary

In this lesson, you inserted tables and borrowed content from other sources. Making use of previously created information sources is an efficient way to publicize that content more widely and to make your site richer with data. You will seek further efficiencies now to reuse some of the content and elements on existing pages to create new ones.

What are some of the benefits of being able to import existing content into Dreamweaver?

What might you want to avoid when adding background color to table cells?

 Note: Check your LogicalCHOICE Course screen for opportunities to interact with your classmates, peers, and the larger LogicalCHOICE online community about the topics covered in this course or other topics you are interested in. From the Course screen you can also access available resources for a more continuous learning experience.

7 Creating Reusable Site Assets

Lesson Time: 45 minutes

Lesson Objectives

In this lesson, you will:

- Create reusable site assets.

- Modify and update Library items.

- Create and use page templates.

Lesson Introduction

You can save considerable time by identifying reusable components on your site pages, storing them in the **Assets Library** panel, and reusing them. New pages can be created by using templates, preserving the look and feel of the site. The focal point for reusability is the **Assets Library** panel.

TOPIC A

Create Reusable Site Assets

As you fashion the various pages for the site, you should review the components and elements you create for potential reuse. By placing items you are likely to use a second time in the **Assets Library** panel, you enable them to be used on new pages. If it becomes necessary to change the library item, you can modify it. When you save the modifications, you are given the option to update all of the copies used on other pages.

Create and Use Reusable Assets

The purpose of the **Assets** panel is to store items used in the website. Because hundreds of components come together to fabricate a site, it is difficult to remember where items were used or placed should you wish to find them. Selecting and storing page components is simple. The **Assets** panel automatically stores many of the items used on the pages, including images, colors, external links, multimedia, and JavaScript scripts. If you create one or more page templates, they will be stored in the **Assets** panel. In addition, you can store any special construction you create as a library item. You need only select the item and save it in the library.

Figure 7-1: The Assets panel with the Library chosen.

Find and Create Library Items from Site Pages

The **Assets Library** panel can store existing elements and those that have been newly created. Review the pages that you created for page elements and blocks of text that may be reused. To store an item, open the **Assets** panel, select the **Library** icon, select the page element, and drag it to the **Library** list of items or select the **New Item** button.

Use Library Items on Site Pages

Using Library items is equally straightforward. They can be dragged from the Library to the location on the page. Alternatively, you can place the insertion point, select the item in the Library, and select the **Insert** button.

 Access the Checklist tile on your LogicalCHOICE course screen for reference information and job aids on How to Store Reusable Assets

ACTIVITY 7–1
Finding and Creating Library Items from Site Pages

Data File

olive_oil.html

Scenario

You have more pages to construct for the website and you would like to take advantage of as many time savers you can. You would like to save some page elements in the Assets Library panel so you can use them again. You will use the library items to complete a page.

1. Create a new site for this lesson.
   a) Select **Site→ New Site**.
   b) In the **Site Setup for Unnamed Site** dialog box, in the **Site Name** text box, type the site name, *7EE*

2. Identify the site root folder.

   a) To the right of the **Local Browse Folder** text box, select the **Browse for folder** 📁 icon.
   b) In the **Choose Root Folder** dialog box, navigate to the **C:\092001Data\Creating Reusable Site Assets** folder.
   c) Select the **Open** button and select the **Select** button.

3. Create and identify the **graphics** folder.
   a) In the **Site Setup for 7EE** dialog box, select **Advanced Settings**.

   b) To the right of the **Default Images folder** text box, select the **Browse for folder** 📁 icon.
   c) Select the **graphics** folder.
   d) Select the **Open** button.
   e) Select the **Select** button.

4. Save the site and confirm the listing of the site folders.
   a) Select the **Save** button.
   b) In the **Files** panel, note the site root folder **Creating Reusable Site Assets** and the **graphics** folder.

5. View completed pages for reusable assets and add them to the library.
   a) Open the **index.html** file.

   b) Select the **Assets** panel tab and select the **Library** 📖 icon.

   c) Select the **banner** graphic and select the **New Library Item** 🔲 icon at the bottom edge of the **Library** panel.
   d) In the **Dreamweaver** dialog box, select **OK**.
   e) In the **Name** column of the **Library** panel, type *ee_banner* and press **Enter**.
   f) If the **Update Files** dialog box appears, select the **Update** button.
   g) In the footer section, select all the footer text.
   h) Select the **New Library Item** icon.
   i) In the **Name** column of the **Library** panel, type *copyright* and press **Enter**.
   j) Save the file.

k) Close all open files.

6. Open a page that needs completion and insert the library items required.
   a) Select the **Files** panel and open the **olive_oil.html** file.
   b) Place the insertion point in the header area at the top left of the page.
   c) Open the **Assets** panel and be sure the **Library** icon is selected.
   d) Select the **ee_banner**.
   e) At the bottom of the **Library** panel, select the **Insert** button.
   f) Select in the body of the page to deselect the banner.

7. Insert a text library item on the page.
   a) Place the insertion point in the footer.
   b) In the **Assets Library** panel, select the **copyright** item.
   c) At the bottom of the **Library** panel, select the **Insert** button.
   d) Click in the body of the page to deselect the footer text.
   e) Save the file as *my_olive_oil.html* and leave it open for the next activity. Close **olive_oil.html**.

8. Place a library item in a second page.
   a) Select the **Files** panel and open the file **harvest.html**.
   b) Place the insertion point in the footer.
   c) In the **Assets** panel, select the **Library** icon, and select the **copyright** item.
   d) At the bottom of the **Library** panel, select the **Insert** button.
   e) Click in the body of the page to deselect the footer text.
   f) Save the file as *my_harvest.html* and leave it open for the next activity. Close **harvest.html**.

TOPIC B

Modify and Update Library Items

The true value and power of library items surface when you need to modify an item. If the item is used on several pages, you'll probably want each instance of the item to be updated. If the item wasn't stored in the Library, you would have to change each instance individually, which would take some time and might lead to errors.

Modifying and Updating Library Items

When a library item is changed, you have the choice to update all copies of the item used on other pages and Dreamweaver performs that procedure for you.

Access the Checklist tile on your LogicalCHOICE course screen for reference information and job aids on How to Edit Library Items

ACTIVITY 7-2
Modifying and Updating Library Items

Before You Begin

The files my_olive_oil.html and my_harvest.html are open.

Scenario

The footer text you placed on the page needs some enhancement. You will add a special symbol to the library item so that whenever it is used, it will have the same look and feel.

Modify the footer text library item.

a) In the **Assets** panel, select the **Library** icon and select the **copyright** item.

b) At the bottom of the **Library** panel, select the **Edit** icon.

c) In the **Copyright.lbi** document, place the insertion point after the word "Copyright."

d) Press the **Spacebar**.

e) On the **Application** bar, select **Insert→HTML→Special Characters→Copyright**.

f) Press the **Spacebar**.

g) Save the **copyright.lbi** file.

h) In the **Update Library Items** dialog box, review the pages to be updated and select the **Update** button.

i) If the **Update Pages** dialog box appears, select the **Close** button.

j) Close the .lbi file.

k) Note that the copyright symbol has been added to the footer text in the **my_harvest.html** page.

l) Click the document tab for **my_olive_oil.html** and inspect the footer text to confirm that the copyright symbol was updated on that page as well.

m) Save and close all files.

TOPIC C

Create and Use Page Templates

You would prefer it if all your web pages were unique and interesting to the visitor. However, you know that there is wisdom in making the structure similar from page to page. Consistent structure gives the reader reassurance that navigation from page to page will not bring up surprises and confusion. Dreamweaver templates are a perfect solution for constructing pages with similar construction. With a template, the basic layout of the page can be created with little effort. You will devote your attention instead to adding the unique content for that page.

Creating and Using Page Templates

Creating a template fixes the structure and graphic nature of the page, but allows the entry of variable content that makes the page unique. You will be able to spend appropriate time on the variable content for the new page as opposed to wasting time creating a page structure identical to the prototype page.

Starter Layouts

Starter layouts are pre-defined layouts with navigation buttons, placeholder logo, dimensions, and color coding. They are listed in the **New Document** dialog box and when you select each layout, the right pane displays the preview and description of the selected item. You can use these layouts as templates to create web pages.

The Nature of Templates

Templates can be basic with a simple page structure or they can be copies of the most intricate page structure used on the site. In Dreamweaver, you can create as many templates as you need. You can have a simple template with just a header and body and another with header, footer, sidebar, and content area as well.

Advantages of Templates

You can use a template for as many pages as you require. They also preclude accidental modification of the page since the fixed portions of the template cannot be accidentally changed. However, if a change to the template is required at some later date, it can easily be done and the modification will be applied to every page constructed from the template. Templates are both efficient and consistent time savers for the web practitioner.

Template Regions

The elements in the template when created are locked. They can only be changed when the template is open for modification. In order to provide areas of the template where you can enter variable page content, Dreamweaver has several regions. These regions are inserted in the template when constructing it.

Editable Regions

An *editable region* is an area in the template where any content can be placed or created. This area will expand as more content is added. You can use it for text, graphics, tables, lists, headings, or any combination. You can have as many editable regions as you need in a template.

Repeatable Regions/Tables

An area suitable for multiple entries such as catalog items, FAQs, events, or product/service lists is the repeatable region/table. The creator of the page inserts as many rows as required when completing the page.

Optional Regions/Editable Optional Regions

As the page author, you will use the optional regions to show or hide specific content at different times. The editable optional region is where you will show or hide content depending on the situation, but the content is editable at the time you make the decision about what to hide or show.

Creating Templates

You create a template from two potential sources. You can create a template from a blank page by adding text, graphics, and colors, eventually saving it as a template. The second option is to start with a page in the site that has the layout and content you want to repeat and convert it into a template. In the second instance, all variable content must be removed and editable regions must be added, in which the content for the new pages will be entered.

Applying Templates

Templates are stored in a templates folder in the site root folder. Using a template requires only that you choose the template as the basis for a new page after selecting **File→New**.

Detaching a Page Template from a Page

If you wish to detach a page from a template, it can be done. At that point the page becomes a standard web page and every component on the page becomes editable. Also, any subsequent changes to the template will not update the detached page.

Creating Reusable Assets

If you wish to add a number of items with similar structure in a page created with a template, consider adding a repeating region to the template. It enables the entry of multiple lines of data such as part numbers and descriptions. However, just adding a repeating region is not sufficient because it is not an editable region. For the content in a repeating region to be editable, an editable region must be inserted into the repeating region.

Access the Checklist tile on your LogicalCHOICE course screen for reference information and job aids on How to Create a Page Template

Access the Checklist tile on your LogicalCHOICE course screen for reference information and job aids on How to Use a Page Template

Access the Checklist tile on your LogicalCHOICE course screen for reference information and job aids on How to Detach a Page Template from a Page

ACTIVITY 7–3
Creating a Page Template

Data File

C:\092001Data\Creating Reusable Site Assets\my_olive_oil.html

Scenario

You need to create additional pages. You would like to produce them with the same layout you spent hours constructing when you created the first one. You don't want to spend time building each page from a blank page or a layout. Creating a template will save you hours of time if you clean up an existing page of its variable content and convert it into a template. You decide that the olive oil page is a good candidate for a template.

---

1. Open a page to create a Dreamweaver template from it.
   a) Open the **my_olive_oil.html** file.
   b) Select **File→Save as Template**.
   c) In the **Save As Template** dialog box, in the **Save as** text box, type *ee_basic* and select the **Save** button.
   d) Answer **Yes** to **Update Links**.
   e) Note that the file is now named **ee_basic.dwt** as a Dreamweaver template file.

2. Remove all variable content from the template.
   a) Select the **olive oil** graphic and press **Delete**.
   b) Select the "Olive Oils" heading and the paragraphs below it.
   c) Press **Delete**.
   d) Select the entire definition list and delete it.
   e) Select **File→Save** to save the template.
   f) Select **OK** to the editable regions message.

3. Add editable regions to the template.
   a) Place the insertion point at the top of the white content area.
   b) Select **Insert→Template Objects→Editable Region**.
   c) In the **New Editable Region** dialog box, in the **Name** text box, type *main*
   d) Select **OK**.
   e) Click in the main editable region box.
   f) In the **Properties** panel, be sure the **HTML** button is selected.
   g) Select the **Format** drop-down arrow and change the selection to **None**.
   h) Select the **Code** button.
   i) Delete any heading tags **<h1>**, **<h2>**, or **<h3>** left inside the **<div>** with the class name **content**.

   ```
   <div class="content"> <!-- TemplateBeginEditable name="main"
   -->main<!-- TemplateEndEditable -->
      <h3> </h3>

      <!-- end .content --></div>
   ```

   j) In the **CSS Styles** panel, click the **Refresh** button and select the **Design** button.
   k) Save the template and close it.

ACTIVITY 7–4
Applying a Page Template

Data Files

ee_basic.dwt

events.txt

Scenario

The marketing manager has a list of three new pages she wants for the site. You created a template by using one of your preferred page layouts. You need to test the template by using it to create a new page. If the template works, you will be able to create the three new pages very quickly.

Create a page by using the new template.

a) In the **Welcome Screen**, in the **Create New** column, select the **More** icon.

b) In the **New Document** dialog box, in the first column, select **Page from Template**.

c) In the **Site** column, select the **7EE** site.

d) In **Template for Site7EE**, select the **ee_basic** template.

e) Select the **Create** button.

f) Note the label to the upper right identifying this page as having been created with a template. Also note the editable region with the main tag.

g) Select the **Design** button.

h) Select the word "main" in the editable region, type *Events* and press **Enter**.

i) Open the **Events.txt** file. Copy all of the text, and close the file.

j) Paste the **Events.txt** text in the editable region below the heading.

k) Place the insertion point in the "Events" heading.

l) In the **Properties** panel, be sure the **HTML** button is selected.

m) In the **Format** drop-down menu, select **Heading 1.**

n) Place the insertion point in each of the headings "Olive Picking Holidays," "Olive Festivals," and "Olive Museums" and select **Heading 3** for each.

o) Save the file as *my_events.html* and preview in the browser.

p) Close the browser and all open files.

ACTIVITY 7-5
Creating Reusable Assets (Optional)

Data File

ee_basic.dwt

Scenario

You need a template with a repeatable region for created pages of olive types and other multiple listings. You decide to add a repeatable region to a basic template.

1. Add a repeatable region to the **ee_basic.dwt** template.
   a) In the **Files** panel, open the **ee_basic_dwt** template.
   b) Following the **main** editable region, add a table with the following values:
      - Rows: *2*
      - Columns: *2*
      - Table width: *600* pixels
      - Border thickness: *1*
      - Cell padding: *8*
      - Cell spacing: *3*
      - Header: Top

2. Populate the table.
   a) First column, first row: *Olive Varieties*
   b) Second column, first row: *Descriptions*

3. In the second row of the table, insert a repeating region.
   a) Place the insertion point in a cell in the second row.
   b) In the **Tag Selector**, select the **<tr>** tag to select the entire second row.
   c) Select **Insert→Template Objects→Repeating Region**.
   d) In the **New Repeating Region** dialog box, in the **Name** text box, type *multi_olives* and select **OK**.
   e) If necessary, place the insertion point in a cell in the second row.
   f) In the **Tag Selector**, select the **<tr>** tag to select the entire second row.
   g) Select **Insert→Template Objects→Editable Region**.
   h) In the **New Editable Region** dialog box, in the **Name** text box, type *olives_descr* and select **OK**.
   i) Save the file as a template *my_ee_repeat* and close it.

4. Begin a new page with the template as a basis.
   a) Select **File→New**.
   b) In the **New Document** dialog box, in the first column select **Page from Template**.
   c) In the third column marked **Template for Site "7EE"**, select **my_ee_repeat**.
   d) Select on the **Create** button.
   e) In the second row, first column, type *Kalamata*
   f) In the second row, second column, type *Grown in Western and Central Greece and the Peloponnese, it has a deep purple color and complex fruity flavor.*
   g) Select the **plus** button above the first column to obtain another row.
   h) In the third row, first column, type *Nicoise* and in the second column, type *Only grown in the French Riviera with a low crop yield, they are mostly sold and eaten domestically. These deep brown olives have little flesh with a large pit.*

i)   You could continue typing other varieties you wish to list with their descriptions.

j)   Save the page as *my_olive_varieties.html*

k)   Preview it in the browser.

l)   Close the browser and close the file.

Summary

In this lesson, you found that some of the time spent in creating web content can be saved by selecting components that you can reuse and storing them in the Dreamweaver Library panel. Additional time can be saved by using a template to create pages with consistent design and layout.

What kinds of assets are you likely to reuse often when developing a website?

Can you think of a downside to reusing site assets?

 Note: Check your LogicalCHOICE Course screen for opportunities to interact with your classmates, peers, and the larger LogicalCHOICE online community about the topics covered in this course or other topics you are interested in. From the Course screen you can also access available resources for a more continuous learning experience.

8 | Linking Web Pages

Lesson Time: 1 hour

Lesson Objectives

In this lesson, you will:

- Create common hyperlinks to site pages.

- Build links to page locations.

- Construct email links.

- Produce an image map.

- Construct navigation and rollover buttons.

Lesson Introduction

Hypertext links provide the power of the World Wide Web. Visitors to your site will not be satisfied with the information on the home page alone. They expect to see links inviting them to visit other pages and locations where they can find additional information and graphics about the site's purpose.

TOPIC A

Create Common Hyperlinks to Site Pages

The fundamental purpose of links is to take the site visitor to other pages in the site. The links can originate from website text, graphics, or buttons. Every page will have links and because movement from page to page involves some of the same page destinations, you should plan to create a navigation bar for some pages.

Creating Common Hyperlinks

Links from one page to another within a website are the most common *hypertext links*, or *hyperlinks*. Generally called an *internal link*, they are the simplest to construct and they are the most numerous in a site.

The Anatomy of the Hyperlink

The link built on a portion of text will be blue and underlined. When the link is used to migrate to another page, the color will change to magenta. These are the default text colors of links when first created. By using CSS, you can change the colors, the underlining, and other characteristics of the text to simplify or enhance the appearance of text converted to links.

Four Types of Links

In this lesson, you will create the four types of links possible on web pages: internal, external, named anchor or bookmark, and email links. Each has a different purpose and together they place the site visitor at the center of the entire World Wide Web store of information.

The Role of the Anchor Tag

On the web page, the link appears as colored text or a graphic, but in the code instructions to the browser it is the anchor tag with its attributes that takes the visitor to the link destination. The anchor tag surrounds the link object (text or graphic) and the href attribute provides the destination to which the browser takes the reader.

Use of the anchor tag with a text link:

<a href="destination page or URL" >Text</a>

Use of the anchor tag with an image tag <img> identifying the graphic object:

<a href="destination page"><img src="graphic file" /></a>

You would use the target attribute if you wish to control the window in which the new page appears.

Use of the target attribute:

<a href="destination page or URL" target="_blank" >Text</a>

Target Value	Placement
_blank	Destination document opens in a new window or tab.
_self (default)	Destination document opens in the same window in which it was clicked.
_parent	Destination document opens in the parent frame.

Target Value	Placement
_top	Destination document opens in the full body of the window.

Text Link Styles

Links can be in one of four states. If the link is unused, its state is "link." After it has been clicked and visited, its state is "visited." If a mouse pointer is moved over the link, its state becomes "hover" until the mouse pointer is moved away, when it reverts to the state it was before the hover. Finally, at the moment the link is clicked, its state is "active." The active state of the link is brief, but if the reader holds the mouse button down in the act of clicking it, the browser will display the active state of the link.

You can style text links according to their state by using CSS pseudo-class selectors. They are listed in the following table in the order in which they should be styled to follow the rules of the cascade. The attributes in the second column are the choices of text styling available and generally applied to the text links to change their appearance and to confirm their visited, hover, and active states.

Anchor Pseudo-Class	Typical Styles Used to Display Change of State
a:link	Color for unused links, underlining if desired
a:visited	Color for visited links, underlining if desired
a:hover	Selection from new color, underline, bold, or background color
a:active	Generally not styled but can use variants of styles used for hover

Graphics As Links

Any graphic can be used as a link. Generally, graphics used for links are small in size. Larger graphics are used as the basis for an image map where two or more links are assigned to portions of the image. You will create an image map later in this lesson. When you transform a graphic into a link, the graphic will have a blue border. You can remove the border by using the CSS decoration style for the <img> tag.

The Nature of Internal and External Links

Internal links need only the page file name and its location in the site as the href attribute value. If the destination page is in the same folder as the page from which the link originates, only the page file name is needed. *External links* are links to other websites and they require a full URL, such as **http://www.cnn.com**.

The file:/// Links

If you don't save the web page after creating links, then file:/// <file name> links are temporarily created with the linked file. Once you save the page, the actual link is established with the linked file.

 Access the Checklist tile on your LogicalCHOICE course screen for reference information and job aids on How to Create Internal and External Links

ACTIVITY 8-1
Creating Internal and External Links

Data Files

index.html

history.html

harvest.html

olive_oil.html

world.html

Scenario

The president and the marketing manager are both impressed with your work on the site. They have asked that you provide a few links to other pages and one to the external site of the International Olive Oil Council. You want to get those links in place and demonstrate how well the links work.

1. Create a new site for this lesson.
   a) Select **Site→New Site**.
   b) In the **Site Setup for Unnamed Site** dialog box, in the **Site Name** text box, type the site name, *8EE*

2. Identify the site root folder.
   a) To the right of the **Local Site Folder** text box, select the **Browse for folder** icon.
   b) In the **Choose Root Folder** dialog box, navigate to the **C:\092001Data\ Linking Web Pages** folder.
   c) Select the **Open** button and select the **Select** button.

3. Create and identify the **graphics** folder.
   a) In the **Site Setup for 8EE** dialog box, select **Advanced Settings**.
   b) To the right of the **Default Images folder** text box, select the **Browse for folder** icon.
   c) Select the **graphics** folder.
   d) Select the **Open** button.
   e) Select the **Select** button.

4. Save the site and confirm the listing of the site folders.
   a) Select the **Save** button.
   b) In the **Files** panel, note the site root folder **Linking Web Pages** and the **graphics** and **Templates** folders.

5. Create internal links.
   a) Open the home page, **index.html**.
   b) Select the text "History" in the upper sidebar area.
   c) In the **Properties** panel, be sure the **HTML** button is selected.
   d) To the right of the **Link** text box select the **Browse for File** icon.
   e) In the **Select File** dialog box, select the **history.html** file and select **OK**.
   f) Select the text "Harvesting" in the upper sidebar area.
   g) Select the **Browse for File** icon.
   h) In the **Select File** dialog box, select the **harvest.html** file and select **OK**.

    i)   Select the text "Olive Oil" in the upper sidebar area.

    j)   Select the **Browse for File** icon.

    k)   In the **Select File** dialog box, select the **olive_oil.html** file and select **OK**.

    l)   Save the page and preview it in the browser to test the links.

6. Create an external link.

    a)   Open the **world.html** page.

    b)   In the second paragraph, in the last sentence, select the text "International Olive Council's."

    c)   In the **Properties** panel, in the **Link** text box, type *http://www.internationaloliveoil.org/*

    d)   Select the **Target** drop-down arrow, select **_blank**, and press **Enter**.

    e)   Save the file as *my_world.html*, preview the page in the browser, and test the link.

    f)   Close the browser and all the open files.

TOPIC B

Create Links to Page Locations

Links to other pages will bring the site visitor to the top of the destination page. You also can create a link to a specific location on a page. This is valuable when a long page of information is organized according to specific topics. You can create a simple table of contents at the top of the page and make each item in the table of contents a link to the section of the page that contains the topic information. These links are called *named anchor links* or *bookmark links*.

Create Links to Page Locations

The named anchor link consists of two parts. First, you identify and name the destination on the page by using an anchor tag. Then you create a link to it by using a second anchor tag. You can have as many sets of named anchor links as you wish. They enable the reader to move from topic of interest to the information on that topic and back again.

 Note: For more information about creating links, check out the LearnTO **Select a Method for Completing Links** presentation by clicking the **LearnTO** tile on your LogicalCHOICE Course screen.

Anchor or Bookmark Links

The links to the various locations are generally located at the top of the page. The named destination anchors are where the information is for each topic. You will also provide a named anchor link combination to get the reader from the information back up to the topic listing.

The Components of the Anchor Link

The link at the origin (the table of content entry) will contain a hash mark or pound sign (#) followed by the name used for the named anchor destination as the value of the "href" attribute, as seen in the example below.

<a href="#extra-virgin olive oil">Extra-Virgin Olive Oil</a>

The named anchor in the body of the HTML document will have the name attribute value that matches the anchor at the origin, as the example below demonstrates.

<a name="extra-virgin olive oil">Extra Virgin Olive Oil</a>

You can create a named anchor set to take the reader from one page to another as the generic example below shows. Note in the origin link how the hash mark or pound sign and anchor name follow the web page file name.

At the origin or table of contents: **< a href="http://otherpage.html#newinfo">New Information</a>**

At the destination:**<a name="newinfo">New Information</a>**

 Access the Checklist tile on your LogicalCHOICE course screen for reference information and job aids on How to Create Links to Page Locations

ACTIVITY 8-2
Creating Links to Page Locations

Data File
products.html

Scenario
The marketing manager stopped by to mention that the Products and Services page should be easier for the visitor to navigate. She asked if you could put a list of the products at the top of the page and convert them to links that would bring the visitor down to the specific product. She also suggested it would be a good idea if you gave them a convenient way to get back to the top of the page without having to scroll their way up. You said you would do that next.

---

1. Create named anchors in the products.html page.
   a) Open **products.html**.
   b) In the second row of the Olive Based Products table, in the first column, place the insertion point at the beginning of the text "Olive Oils."
   c) On the **Application** bar, select **Insert→Named Anchor**.
   d) In the **Named Anchor** dialog box, type *olive_oils* and select **OK**.
   e) An anchor icon will appear at the location if **Visual Aids→Invisible Elements** is checked.
   f) In the second row, create a named anchor before the text "Olive Pastes" named *pastes*
   g) In the third row, create a named anchor before the text "Cured Olives" named *cured*

2. Create links to the named anchors.
   a) In the table at the top of the page, select the text "Olive Oils."
   b) In the **Properties** panel, be sure the **HTML** button is selected.
   c) In the **Properties** panel, in the **Link** text box, type *#olive_oils* and press **Enter**.
   d) At the top of the page, select the text "Olive Pastes and Tapenades."
   e) In the **Properties** panel, in the **Link** text box, type *#pastes* and press **Enter**.
   f) At the top of the page, select the text "Cured Olives."
   g) In the **Properties** panel, in the **Link** text box, type *#cured* and press **Enter**.

3. Create a return link to the top of the page.
   a) Select the banner graphic at the top of the page.
   b) Press the left arrow key to move the insertion point to the left of the banner.
   c) Select **Insert→Named Anchor** and name it *top*

4. Create the links to go to the top of the page.
   a) In the second row, third column of the Olive Based Products table, place the insertion point after the last sentence.
   b) Hold down **Shift** and press **Enter**. Type *Top*
   c) Select the word "Top."
   d) In the **Properties** panel, in the **Link** text box, type *#top* and press **Enter**.
   e) Copy the link **Top** and paste it after every product description in the third column.
   f) Save the file as **my_products.html**, preview it in the browser, and check every link.
   g) Leave **my_products.html** open for the next activity. Close the browser and **products.html**.

TOPIC C

Create Email Links

When you create an email link, you are providing a means for your site visitor to contact you directly with the email client application resident on their computer. It is the easiest and quickest method to invite feedback or to ask for information from the reader.

Email Links

When visitors use the *email link*, their default email application provides a blank email form with the email address to which you are directing correspondence. If you create a new email address to receive emails from the website, you must be sure that your email client is configured to receive the new email address.

How Email Links Function

When the visitor chooses to send an email message to the address on the site, the browser engages the email client on the visitor's computer and requests a new email form, filling in the email address from the href attribute value. The reader simply fills in the subject and body of the email message and sends it off. If the email link has a special purpose, such as "Feedback" or "Suggestions on This Topic," you can also specify the subject of the email as well by adding the subject to the href value.

Creating Email Links

An email link with just the recipient address specified would look like this:

`<a href="mailto: marketing @ emeraldepicure .com"> Comments </a>`

An email link with the address and subject specified would look like this:

`<a href="mailto:marketing@emeraldepicure.com?Subject=New Products">New Product Suggestion</a>`

 Access the Checklist tile on your LogicalCHOICE course screen for reference information and job aids on How to Create Email Links

ACTIVITY 8–3
Creating Email Links

Before You Begin
The file my_products.html is open.

Scenario
The president came by and asked if the marketing manager remembered to request an email link on the products page. They had been discussing it and thought it would be a good idea. Their rationale was there are hundreds of products being made with olives in many countries around the world. Customers would regularly see these new products and might want to suggest that Emerald Epicure Ltd. carry them. If you invited them to share information about these new products, Emerald Epicure could research them and expand its product line.

Create an email link.

a) In the table at the top of the page, place the insertion point in the last row.

b) Type *If you have suggestions for new products, contact us: New Product Suggestions*

c) Select the text "New Product Suggestions."

d) In the **Properties** panel, be sure the **HTML** button is selected.

e) In the **Link** text box, type *mailto:marketing@emeraldepicure.com?subject=New Product Suggestion*

f) Save the file, preview it in the browser, and check the email link.

g) Close the browser and **my_products.html**.

TOPIC D

Image Maps and Linking

Image maps are an innovative way to combine a single graphic with multiple links. You will do this by selecting specific areas of the graphic called hot spots and create those areas as links to pages or other websites.

Image Maps and Linking

The *image map* should have two or more areas that can be modified to be *hotspots*. Hotspots are used by the site visitor to navigate to other locations. They function very much as graphics that are links.

Components of the Image Map

The image chosen for an image map must be named uniquely and the hotspots must be drawn by using tools in the **Properties** panel. Once you draw the hotspots, Dreamweaver allows them to accept an anchor tag and an href attribute in which you will identify a page or Web destination. At that point they behave identically to a graphic link.

Hotspots

In the **Properties** panel, the tools for drawing hotspots consist of a **Pointer Hotspot** tool, a **Rectangle Hotspot** tool, a **Circle Hotspot** tool, and a **Polygon Hotspot** tool. These tools enable any shape hotspot to be drawn.

Hotspot Best Practices

The order in which you draw the hotspots determines which has precedence if overlapped. Therefore, the best practice is to create your hotspots so they don't overlap. Slight overlaps will not impede the function of the hotspots because most site visitors tend to click near the center of any image used as a hotspot link.

 Access the Checklist tile on your **LogicalCHOICE** course screen for reference information and job aids on **How to Create an Image Map**

ACTIVITY 8-4
Creating an Image Map

Data File

my_world.html

Scenario

A colleague suggested that an alternate link to the home page and the harvest page might be nice to include. Rather than introduce other graphics, you decide to use the banner on the world page. You will create a rectangular hotspot over the logo, which is to the left of the banner, and direct that link to the index (home) page. You will create a polygonal hotspot over the leaves and olives on the right side of the banner and link it to the harvest page.

1. Open **my_world.html**.

2. Choose the image map, name it, and create the hotspots.
   a) In the **my_world.html** page, select the page banner.
   b) In the **Properties** panel, in the **Map** section's lower left **Map** text box, type *ee_map*
   c) Select the **Rectangle Hotspot** tool.
   d) Begin at the upper left corner above the **ee_banner**. Click and drag a rectangle that covers the entire logo.
   e) In the **Dreamweaver** dialog box reminder about the **'alt'** field, select **OK**.
   f) In the **Alt** text box, type *The Emerald Epicure Logo Hotspot that links to the Home Page*
   g) In the **Link** text box, select the **Browse for File** icon and select **index.html** and select **OK**.
   h) If a hotspot shape requires adjustment, select the **Pointer Hotspot** tool and move the hotspot nodes.
   i) Save the file, preview it in the browser, and test the image map link.
   j) Close the browser and all the files except for **my_world.html**.

TOPIC E

Navigation and Rollovers

You have created the four types of links used on web pages. In most cases, the links were imposed on text, graphics, and text made to look like buttons. Dreamweaver has excellent tools to create *navigation bars*, which are a collection of buttons with rollover effects. Navigation or menu bars are more convenient for the site because they can perform all of the navigation desired with the collection of buttons displayed. They are one of the many Spry objects available in Dreamweaver.

Rollover effects for graphics are another item of interest for the visitor. You can display twice as many graphics by having the in-place graphic rolling over to another image when the reader hovers the mouse pointer over it.

Navigation and Rollovers

Both navigation or menu bars and rollover images are both accomplished with the use of *JavaScript*, a language that conveys interactivity to the web page. JavaScript is understood by browsers and you need not study the language to become adept in its use.

Menu Bar Elements

When you create a **Spry** menu bar, Dreamweaver takes charge and creates the multi-level menu bar in the form you determine. Construction of the buttons is controlled in the **Properties** panel. The menu bar is just a list of links that is styled by CSS. The styling is sophisticated enough for Dreamweaver to segregate it in a separate style sheet and folder called Spry Assets. You will likely change the default colors (gray and purple) because your site will have colors that are different.

Button and Image Rollover Effects

Rollover effects are created by using Dreamweaver's **Insert→Image Objects→Rollover Image** command. It is important to have two images available. If you are using a button image, both images must be the same size. They may have different color or color effects to demonstrate the change in appearance.

Objects Created in Drawing Programs

Individual buttons can be created in other drawing programs and other Adobe applications. For example, buttons can be constructed in Photoshop, Fireworks, Flash, and Illustrator. To be prepared to use the buttons in Dreamweaver, you should be sure you have a minimum of two images, one for the static button and another for the rollover image of the button. In Dreamweaver, they would simply be used as graphic images with a rollover effect applied and linked to the destination page or website.

 Access the Checklist tile on your LogicalCHOICE course screen for reference information and job aids on How to Create a Spry Menu (Navigation) Bar

ACTIVITY 8-5
Creating a Navigation Bar

Before You Begin
The file my_world.html is open.

Scenario
The general wisdom is that everyone who visits the site will want to see the world page to view the production and consumption numbers. The next thing they would likely do is to move off from there to the rest of the site. To give the site visitor the most convenient way to navigate to the other pages, it is suggested that you create a menu or navigation bar on that page that includes links to all of the pages in the site.

1. Create a **Spry** menu bar.
   a) Place the insertion point before the word "World" in the heading at the top of the page.
   b) Press the up arrow key once and confirm you are in the **navbar** area by checking the **Properties** panel **Class** text box.
   c) Select **Insert→Spry→Spry Menu Bar**.
   d) In the **Spry Menu Bar** dialog box, select the **Horizontal** radio button and select **OK**.
   e) You are given four default navigation buttons with two of them having secondary pop-up buttons. The buttons are arranged in the **Properties** panel in three columns.
   f) In the **Properties** panel, the text of the first button is highlighted. The text box to the extreme right is where you edit the text.
   g) In the **Text** box, highlight the text "Item 1," type *Home* and press **Enter**.
   h) In the first column select **Item 2**. In the **Text** box, highlight the text "Item 2," type *Olives* and press **Enter**.
   i) Select **Item 3**, highlight the text "Item 3," type *History* and press **Enter**.
   j) Select **Item 4**, highlight the text "Item 4, " type *World* and press **Enter**.
   k) Above the first column, select the **+**.
   l) In the far right **Text** box, replace the text **Untitled Item** with *About Us* and press **Enter**.
   m) Above the first column select the **+**.
   n) In the far right **Text** box, replace the text "Untitled Item" with *Contact Us* and press **Enter**.

2. Create the second tier of pop-up menu buttons.
   a) In **Properties** panel, in the first column, scroll up and select **Home**.
   b) In the second column, select each item in turn and click the **−** above to delete it.
   c) In the first column, select **Olives**.
   d) In the **second** column, select the **+** and in the **Text** box, replace the text **Untitled Item** with *Harvesting* and press **Enter**.
   e) Select the **+** again, and in the **Text** box, replace the text **Untitled Item** with *Olive Oil* and press **Enter**.
   f) Select the **+** again, and in the **Text** box, replace the text **Untitled Item** with *Products* and press **Enter**.
   g) In **Properties** panel, in the first column, select **History**.
   h) In the second column, select each item in turn and click the **−** (minus sign) above to delete it.
   i) In the **Dreamweaver** dialog box, select **OK**.
   j) In **Properties** panel, in the first column, select **World**.
   k) In the second column, select the **+** and, in the **Text** box replace the text **Untitled Item** with *Events* and press **Enter**

3. Create the links for the buttons.

a) In **Properties** panel, in the first column, select **Home**.

b) At the far end of the **Link** text box, select the **Browse** folder icon.

c) In the **Select File** dialog box, select the **index.html** file and select **OK**.

d) In the first column, select **Olives** and, in the second column, select **Harvesting**.

e) Select the **Browse** folder icon, select the **harvest.html** file, and select **OK**.

f) In the second column select **Olive Oil**, select the **Browse** icon, and select **olive_oil.html** and select **OK**.

g) In the second column, select **Products**, select the **Browse** icon, and select **products.html** and select **OK**.

h) In the first column, select **History**, select the **Browse** icon, and select **history.html** and select **OK**.

i) In the first column, select **World** and be sure the **Link** text box has a **#** in it.

j) In the second column, select **Events**, select the **Browse** icon, and select **events.html** and select **OK**.

k) Save the file.

l) Note that Dreamweaver will create a separate folder with all the files supporting the menu bar.

m) In the **Copy Dependent Files** dialog box, select **OK**.

n) Preview **my_world.html** in the browser and note that the browser may block the menu bar from running.

o) Unblock the file if necessary and check the links.

p) Close the browser and **my_world.html**.

 Access the Checklist tile on your LogicalCHOICE course screen for reference information and job aids on How to Create an Image Rollover

ACTIVITY 8-6
Creating an Image Rollover

Data Files

events.html

tuscan_farm.jpg

tuscan_hills.jpg

Scenario

Your events page is undecorated and some of your colleagues suggested placing an event location picture on the page. Some even suggested a slide show. You don't have time to assemble a slide show but you can place an image and rollover combination.

Create a rollover image.

a) From the **Files** panel, double-click the **events.html** file.

b) Place the insertion point to the left of the word "You" in the first paragraph.

c) Select **Insert→Image Objects→Rollover Image**.

d) In the **Image name** text box, type *events*

e) Select the **Browse** button to the right of the **Original image** text box.

f) From the **Original Image** dialog box, navigate to the **graphics** folder and select the **tuscan_farm.jpg** image.

g) Select **OK**.

h) Select the **Browse** button to the right of the **Rollover image** text box.

i) From the **Rollover Image** dialog box, select the **tuscan_hills.jpg** image.

j) Select **OK**.

k) Be sure the **Preload rollover image** check box is checked.

l) In the **Alternate text** box, type *Olive Events and Venues*

m) Select **OK** and save the file as *my_events.html*

n) In the **Document** bar, select the **Live** button and hover over the image with the mouse.

o) Select the **Live** button again to disable it.

p) Preview in the browser and, if necessary, allow blocked content.

q) Hover over the image with the mouse pointer.

r) Close the browser and close all files.

ACTIVITY 8–7
Linking Web Pages (Optional)

Data File

ee_basic.dwt

Scenario

You would like to add a Spry menu bar to the basic template to make it more versatile for creating pages.

1. Open the template and add the **Spry** menu bar.
   a) In the **Files** panel, in the **Templates** folder, double-click **ee_basic.dwt** to open it.
   b) Save it as *my_ee_navbar.dwt*
   c) Select the **Code** button and place the insertion point on blank line **128** to select the **navbar** region.
   d) Select the **Design** button and confirm that the **Properties** panel indicates the **navbar** class is shown.
   e) Select **Insert→Spry→Spry Menu Bar**.
   f) In the **Spry Menu Bar** dialog box, be sure the **Horizontal** option is chosen and select **OK**.
   g) In the **Properties** panel, in the **second** column of menu items, delete items **1.1** through **1.3** by selecting them and selecting the **minus** sign above the column.
   h) In column 1, be sure **Item 1** is selected. In the **Text** box to the right, select **Item 1** and type *Home*
   i) In the **Link** text box below, type *index.html*
   j) In column 1 be sure **Item 2** is selected. In the **Text** box to the right, select **Item 2**, type *Olives* and press **Enter**.
   k) Above column 2, click the **plus** icon for a new item and, in the **Text** box to the right, type *Harvesting*
   l) In the **Link** box, type *harvest.html* and press **Enter**.
   m) Repeat steps k and l for **Products** and **products.html** and press **Enter** when done.
   n) In column 1, select **Item 3** and, in the second column, delete items **3.1** through **3.3**.

    Note: If a dialog box pops up during this deletion warning about third level menu items, select **OK** and continue.

   o) In the **Text** box for **Item 3**, type *World* and in the **Link** text box, type *world.html*
   p) In column 1 select **Item 4**. In the **Text** box, type *History* and, in the **Link** text box, type *history.html*
   q) Save the file.

2. Format the **Spry Menu Bar** buttons.
   a) In the **CSS Styles** panel, select the **All** button.
   b) Scroll to the bottom of the **All Rules** section to locate the **SpryMenuBarHorizontal.css** style sheet.
   c) Select the **plus** to the left of the style sheet and scroll down to see the styles better.
   d) Select the **ul.MenuBarHorizontal a** style.
   e) In the **Properties for "ul.MenuBarHorizontal a"** select the color value for the **background-color**.
   f) Type *#066700*
   g) Select the color value for the **color** style, type *#FFD301* and press **Enter**.
   h) In the **All Rules** section, select the **ul.MenuBarHorizontal a:hover, ul.MenuBarHorizontal a:focus** style.
   i) In the **Properties for** listing, select the color value for the **background-color**.
   j) Type *#FFD301*
   k) Select the color value for the **color** style, type *#066700* and press **Enter**.

l) In the **All Rules** section, select the **ul.MenuBarHorizontal a.MenuBarItemHover, ul.MenuBarHorizontal a.MenuBarItemSubmenuHover, ul.MenuBarHorizontal a.MenuBarSubmenuVisible** style.

m) In the **Properties for** listing, select the color value for the **background-color**.

n) Type *#FFD301*

o) Select the color value for the **color** style, type *#066700* and press **Enter**.

p) Save the file and close the template. If prompted to save changes to the CSS, select **Yes**.

3. Create a page from the template and test the **Spry** menu bar.

a) Select **File→New**.

b) In the **New Document** dialog box, in the first column, select **Page from Template**.

c) In the third column marked **Template for Site "8EE"**, select **my_ee_navbar**.

d) Select the **Create** button.

e) On the **Document** bar, select the **Live** button.

f) Hover the mouse pointer over each button.

g) Note how the colors change and how the second button displays the secondary menu choices.

h) Select the **Live** button to turn it off.

i) Save the page as *my_spry_menu.html*

j) Preview the page in the browser to check the links. Be sure to turn off any browser security blocking before testing.

k) Select the **Home** button and others to check the links.

l) Use the browser **Back** button to get back to your Spry menu page.

m) Close the browser and close all open files.

Summary

In this lesson, you created all of the links the browser supports. You created navigation links to other pages, an external web link, named anchor links, and an email link. You created a Spry menu bar and a rollover image. All of these elements are the motive force behind your website.

Other than visual appeal and for navigating to a large number of pages, can you think of a reason a website developer would prefer to use a menu bar over hypertext links?

What benefit do rollover states present to website visitors?

 Note: Check your LogicalCHOICE Course screen for opportunities to interact with your classmates, peers, and the larger LogicalCHOICE online community about the topics covered in this course or other topics you are interested in. From the Course screen you can also access available resources for a more continuous learning experience.

9 Sending the Website to the Web Server

Lesson Time: 1 hour

Lesson Objectives

In this lesson, you will:

- Validate the website.

- Upload files to the web server.

Lesson Introduction

When your website is complete, you'll want to send the files to the web server to be made available for the world to see. The web server will host the site. The owner of the server may be your organization or it may be a contract Internet Service Provider (ISP). Dreamweaver has all of the tools for transferring the files. The server may be remote from your location. For that reason, *File Transfer Protocol (FTP)* is commonly used to transfer the documents to the server. Dreamweaver has a built-in FTP utility for that function.

To ensure that your site visitors have access to well-constructed pages that operate as intended, you should validate your content prior to uploading the site. This too can be done conveniently within Dreamweaver.

TOPIC A

Validate the Website

You have been careful to construct your site so all of the elements work correctly with the browser. You've viewed each page when completed. With pages consisting of so many elements all of which need to work together and to work with various browsers, it is wise to run the site through a variety of checks before sending the files up to the Web server. Validating your site consists of reviews of your content. These checks are done using various panels and menu choices.

Validating the Website

To perform a thorough check of your site, check the following:

- Spelling
- Links
- Selected site reports
- XHTML HTML validation
- CSS validation
- Cross-browser testing

Spelling

Checking the spelling in your website documents is as easy to accomplish in Dreamweaver as it is in most other programs. Not performing it can lead to serious embarrassment, questionable professionalism, and lack of site credibility. In the rush to complete a site, everyone will leave a typo or two behind. Always perform a spelling check.

Links

Your site's functionality depends on its entire collection of links working correctly. When files or graphics are moved or page names are changed, Dreamweaver does a good job of correcting the links. Many times, though, changes may have been made in haste and corrections can be missed. Check your site for broken and orphan links.

Site Reports

Site reports may be requested at any time. Some site reports deal with workflow issues. These can be helpful when collaborating with a team as you develop a website. Workflow reports can indicate who has checked out a particular file, if certain files have design notes, and which files have been recently modified.

Other reports uncover oversights by checking XHTML attributes. These reports look for issues such as missing Alt text and untitled documents.

XHTML HTML Validation

Whether your documents use HTML or XHTML depends on your choice when creating new documents. The default in Dreamweaver CS6 is XHTML 1.0 Transitional. The DocType (document type) choice in the New Document dialog box determines if the older HTML or the newer XHTML is used. Because they are similar, with XHTML having slightly stricter syntax, they can each be validated with the same tool. The sanctioning body for most web technologies is the World Wide Web Consortium, commonly referred to as the W3C (**http://www.w3.org/**). They supply various validation tools, one of which is for validating HTML or XHTML in web documents.

You can send the page to be validated in three ways. You can supply the URI (Universal Resource Identifier), that is, the Web URL address complete to the page location. You can locate the file on your computer or you can copy the code from your entire page and paste it in a text box on the

Web. When you validate documents, you are encouraged to use a W3C valid icon as testimony to the care and professionalism practiced to create it.

CSS Validation

Your styles can be validated by the W3C as well. When a page is validated for CSS the W3C offers a valid CSS icon as well. In your travels through the WWW, you may see certain sites proudly displaying the W3C icons confirming well-crafted pages.

Cross-Browser Testing

If you will develop and maintain one or more websites, you are encouraged to download all of the popular browsers and install them on your work computer. This allows testing site documents conveniently. Although this is a good practice, you cannot possibly have all of the browsers on your computer that the public uses. That would require all PC browsers, all Mac browsers and all of the new and old versions of these browsers, which are on the numerous computers around the world. Obviously, that is impossible to do.

Adobe has therefore provided us with a Browser Lab service. You need to sign up for a free Adobe account and after signing in you may select a Browser Set of versions you do not have on your computer. The service will create screenshots of your page which you can compare with tools provided.

 Access the Checklist tile on your LogicalCHOICE course screen for reference information and job aids on How to Check Spelling

 Access the Checklist tile on your LogicalCHOICE course screen for reference information and job aids on How to Check Links

 Access the Checklist tile on your LogicalCHOICE course screen for reference information and job aids on How to Check for Orphans

 Access the Checklist tile on your LogicalCHOICE course screen for reference information and job aids on How to Run Reports

ACTIVITY 9-1
Checking Spelling, Links, and Running Reports

Data Files

events.html

olive_oil.html

history.html

harvest.html

Scenario

In preparation for moving the site files up to the web server, you want to be sure there are no errors. You decide to take care of spelling first. You have checked most pages already but you haven't done so with the Events.html file. Next on the list is to check for problems with links for the whole site. Then you will run two reports to check if every graphic in the site has alternate text and that every page has a proper title.

---

1. Create a new site for this lesson.
   a) Select **Site→New Site**.
   b) In the **Site Setup for Unnamed Site** dialog box, in the **Site Name** text box, type the site name, *9EE*

2. Identify the site root folder.

   a) To the right of the **Local Site Folder** text box, select the **Browse for folder** 📁 icon.
   b) In the **Choose Root Folder** dialog box, navigate to the **C:\092001Data\Sending the Website to the Web Server** folder.
   c) Select the **Open** button and select the **Select** button.

3. Create and identify the **graphics** folder.
   a) In the **Site Setup for 8EE** dialog box, select **Advanced Settings**.

   b) To the right of the **Default Images folder** text box, select the **Browse for folder** 📁 icon.
   c) Select the **graphics** folder.
   d) Select the **Open** button.
   e) Select the **Select** button.

4. Save the site and confirm the listing of the site folders.
   a) Select the **Save** button.
   b) In the **Files** panel, note the site root folder **Sending the Website to the Web Server** and the **graphics** folder.

5. Check spelling in the event.html file.
   a) Open **events.html**.
   b) Place the insertion point just before the heading "Events."
   c) Select **Commands→Check Spelling**.
   d) In the **Check Spelling** dialog box, in the **Word not found in dictionary** text box, the word "relagated" is spelled incorrectly.
   e) The **Change to** box shows the correct spelling, select the **Change** button.
   f) The word "occuring" is incorrect. The **Change to** box is correct, so select the **Change** button.
   g) The word "prticipate" is incorrect. The **Change to** box is correct, so select the **Change** button.

---

h) If necessary, the word "millennia" is correct, so select the **Ignore** button.

i) In the **Dreamweaver** dialog box, select **OK**.

6. Check the site for link errors.

a) Select **Site→Check Links Sitewide**.

b) The **Link Checker** panel opens with all **Broken Links** shown.

c) In the **Link Checker** panel, to the right of **events.html**, click the broken link path and select the **Browse for File** icon to the right.

d) In the **Select File** window, browse until you find the correct **tuscan_hills.jpg** file in the graphics folder.

e) Select the thumbnail then click **OK**.

f) In the **Link Checker** panel, click on the whitespace and see the broken link disappear.

g) In the **Link Checker** panel, double-click **olive_oil.html**.

h) On the **olive_oil.html** page, in the upper left, click "History" in the navigation bar.

i) In the **Properties** panel, in the **Link** text box, delete the extra **S** so that "hisstory.html" reads "history.html" and press **Enter**.

j) Save **olive_oil.html** and close the file.

k) Back in **events.html**, in the **Link Checker** panel, to the right of **olive_oil.html**, select the **Browse for File** icon to the right of the broken link.

l) In the **Select File** window, browse until you find the correct **history.html** file.

m) Select the **history.html** icon then click **OK**.

n) In the **Link Checker** panel, click on the whitespace and see the broken link disappear.

o) Save the **events.html** file, and preview it in the browser and check the corrected graphic link. Then close the browser.

7. Check for orphans.

a) On the **Link Checker** tab, select the **Show** drop-down arrow and select **Orphaned Files**.

b) You will find a graphic file that is unused (no page in the site is linked to the graphic).

c) If you were considering a link to this graphic, you would leave it. If not, you would delete it or move it to another folder.

8. Run the Missing Alt Text and Untitled Documents reports.

a) Select the **Site Reports** tab.

b) In the **Site Reports** panel, select the **Reports** drop-down ▷ icon.

c) In the **Reports** dialog box, from the **Report on** drop-down list, select **Entire Current Local Site**.

d) Check the **Missing Alt Text** and **Untitled Documents** check boxes and select **Run**.

e) In the **Site Reports** panel, double-click **events.html**.

f) In the **Properties** panel, in the **Alt** text box, type *Olive Events and Venues* and press **Enter**.

g) In the **Document** bar, select the **Design** button and save the file.

h) In the **Site Reports** panel, double-click the **harvest.html** file.

i) In the **Properties** panel, in the **Title** text box, type *Harvesting Olive Crops* and press **Enter**.

j) Select the **Design** button and save the file.

k) To close the **Site Reports** panel group, select the **Panel Options Menu** icon in the upper right and select **Close Tab Group**.

l) Close all open files.

 Access the Checklist tile on your LogicalCHOICE course screen for reference information and job aids on **How to Check XHTML and HTML**

ACTIVITY 9–2
Checking XHTML and HTML

Data File

C:\092001Data\Sending the Website to the Web Server\harvest.html

Scenario

The marketing manager was looking over the pages you created and suspects one of the pages may have some errors. She suggested you check the XHTML/HTML markup and the CSS styling before you send it to the web server. You noted a strange item on one page and you decide to check it.

Check the suspected page by using the W3C Markup Validation Service.

a) Open the browser and go to the validation site, *http://validator.w3.org/*

b) In the **W3C Markup Validation Service** web page, select the **Validate by File Upload** tab.

c) Select the **Browse** button.

d) In the **Choose File to Upload** dialog box, navigate to the **C:\092001Data\Sending the Website to the Web Server** directory and select the file **harvest.html**.

e) Select the **Open** button.

f) Select the **Check** button.

g) Scroll down the page and note the errors listed. Note the line number of the first error listed. Keep the browser open.

h) Switch to **Dreamweaver** and open **harvest.html**.

i) Select the **Code** button and move to line **170** as noted in the error listing.

j) Correct the **<bodyy>** tag to read **<body>**.

k) Move to line **175** and move the closing **</a>** tag to the end of the text **Home**.

Error listing:	<li><a href="index.html">Home**</li></a**
Correction:	<li><a href="index.html">Home**</a></li**

l) Save the file and recheck the page by performing steps c through f again. (Switch to the web browser and select the **Back** button.)

m) Leave the file open for the next activity.

 Access the Checklist tile on your LogicalCHOICE course screen for reference information and job aids on How to Check CSS Style Rules

ACTIVITY 9-3
Checking CSS Style Rules

Before You Begin
The file harvest.html is open.

Scenario
The marketing manager came by to remind you that the suspected page needed the CSS to be verified as well. You assured her that you would be doing so very shortly.

Check the CSS on the suspected page by using the W3C CSS Validation Service.

a) Open the browser, if necessary, and go to the validation site, *http://jigsaw.w3.org/css-validator/*

b) In the **W3C CSS Validation Service** web page, select the **By file upload** tab.

c) Select the **Browse** button.

d) In the **Choose File to Upload** dialog box, navigate to the **C:\092001Data\Sending the Website to the Web Server** directory and select the file **harvest.html**.

e) Select the **Open** button.

f) Select the **Check** button.

g) Scroll down the page and note the errors listed. Note the line number of the errors listed. Keep the browser open.

h) Switch to **Dreamweaver** and the **harvest.html** file.

i) In the **Code** view, move to line **77** as noted in the error listing.

j) Notice that the three styles under the **.content** selector have **hyphens** (-) separating the styles from their values.

k) There should be **colons** (:) instead. Remove the **hyphens** for each of the three styles and type **colons** instead. When corrected, they should appear as:

```
.content {
    padding: 10px 0;
    width: 80%;
    float: left;
}
```

l) Save the file.

m) Recheck the page.

n) Close the browser and all open files.

TOPIC B

Upload Files to the Web Server

When your website is complete or complete enough to have your audience see it, you will send the site to the web server. You can always add to the site or modify the information. The web server may be hosted by an ISP or your organization.

Upload Files to the Web Server

With Dreamweaver, you can send the whole website root folder to the server or individual files. Obviously, when you have completed a new site, you will send the site to the server for the first time. If you are modifying or creating a new page you will add the updated content to your site.

The Role of Web Hosting

The *web server* is the repository of the website and includes all of its files. These files are the pages you created and all of the supporting elements such as the graphics, CSS styles, and any JavaScript files that Dreamweaver created. In addition to storing the files and protecting them from harm, the web server has a high speed connection to the WWW and answers all requests for your site pages from visitors.

Connecting to a Remote Server

In order for you to transfer the site and later individual pages to the server, you must make a connection to the server within Dreamweaver. This is the most convenient method to transfer files.

Using the Files Panel to Upload the Site

Once the connection information is entered into Dreamweaver, the connection to the site is

accomplished simply by selecting the **Connection** icon in the **Files** panel. The **Files** panel is then expanded to display the local files and the files on the remote web server and the site folder or individual files are downloaded from the server for modification or uploaded to the server.

 Access the Checklist tile on your LogicalCHOICE course screen for reference information and job aids on How to Identify the Remote Web Server

 Access the Checklist tile on your LogicalCHOICE course screen for reference information and job aids on How to Upload Files to the Web Server

ACTIVITY 9–4
Identifying the Remote Server

Before You Begin

Dreamweaver is open.

Scenario

Both the president and the marketing manager are aware that you are close to completion of the site. They requested that you send the files up to the web server so the site can be viewed as a visitor will see it.

1. Create the Remote Server folder.
   a) Hold down the **Windows** key and press **D** to go to the Desktop.
   b) Right-click the **Desktop** and select **New→Folder**.
   c) Rename the folder by typing *My Remote Web Server* and press **Enter**. This folder will represent your **Remote Web Server** folder.
   d) Switch to **Dreamweaver**.

2. Identify the **Remote Web Server** folder for Dreamweaver.
   a) Select **Site→Manage Sites**.
   b) Select your **9EE** site and select the **Edit the currently selected site** 🖉 icon below the listing.
   c) In the category listing on the left, select **Servers**.
   d) Below the server list on the right, select the **Add new Server** ➕ icon.

    Note: Because you are simulating a remote web server, you will make selections guiding Dreamweaver to the folder created on your Desktop. It will represent the web server and all file transfers will simulate uploading your site files to the server.

   e) In the **Server Name** text box, type *My Web Server*
   f) In the **Connect using** drop-down list, select **Local/Network**.
   g) To the right of the **Server Folder** text box, select the **Browse** 📁 icon.
   h) In the **Choose Folder** dialog box, select the **Desktop** icon in the left column.
   i) Select the **My Remote Web Server** folder and select the **Open** button.
   j) Select the **Select** button.
   k) Select the **Save** button.
   l) In the **Site Setup for 9EE** dialog box, select the **Save** button and the **Done** button.

ACTIVITY 9–5
Uploading the Site Files

Before You Begin
Dreamweaver is open.

Scenario
You have set up the Remote Server folder and you are ready to upload the entire website to the server.

Uploading the website to the web server.

a) In the **Files** panel, select the **Connect to Remote Server** icon.

b) Note that the icon appears in color with a green dot when the connection is made.

c) Select the **Expand to show local and remote sites** icon.

d) The screen displays an empty **Remote Server** folder on the left and your local site folder on the right.

e) Because you want to upload the entire site, select the **Site** root folder at the top of the **Local Files** listing on the right.

f) Select the **Put file(s) to "Remote Server"** icon.

g) In the **Dreamweaver** dialog box, select **OK**.

h) Note that all of the files from **Local Files** were transferred to the **Remote Server**.

i) Select the **Collapse to show only local or remote site** icon.

j) Select the **Disconnect from Remote Server** icon.

> Access the Checklist tile on your LogicalCHOICE course screen for reference information and job aids on **How to Download a Web Page for Modification**

ACTIVITY 9-6
Downloading a Web Page for Modifications

Before You Begin
Dreamweaver is open.

Data File
C:\092001Data\Sending the Website to the Web Server\products.html

Scenario
A colleague has detected an error on one of the pages and suggested you correct it before too long. You know it is convenient to download the file and correct the error in Dreamweaver, so you decide to do that now.

Download the file that requires modification.

a) In the **Files** panel select the **Connect to Remote Server** icon.

b) Select the **Expand to show local and remote sites** icon.

c) In the expanded **Remote Server** listing, select the **products.html** file.

d) Select the **Get file(s) from "Remote Server"** icon.

e) In the Dependent Files window, select **Yes**.

f) Select the **Collapse to show only local or remote site** icon.

g) Select the **Disconnect from Remote Server** icon.

h) In **Dreamweaver**, open the **products.html** page and select **Design** view.

i) In the third sentence of the first paragraph, add the text *Ltd.* After "Emerald Epicure."

j) Save and close the file.

k) Reconnect to the **Remote Server**, expand the view, and upload (Put) the file to the **Remote Server**.

l) Collapse the view and disconnect from the **Remote Server**.

Summary

In this lesson, you validated the important qualities of your site, the code, the links and the styling. You also found how expedient it is to connect to your remote web server no matter where it is and manage the transfer of files to and from the server.

Why might it be advantageous to expand the view of the Files panel?

Do you think it's more important for a website developer to push a site live, or to be cautious about running all checks and validations? How do you think you would handle pressure from a client to go live before you feel your website is ready?

 Note: Check your LogicalCHOICE Course screen for opportunities to interact with your classmates, peers, and the larger LogicalCHOICE online community about the topics covered in this course or other topics you are interested in. From the Course screen you can also access available resources for a more continuous learning experience.

Course Follow-Up

In this course, you became familiar with one of the most versatile and professional tools for creating websites. You first identified the workspace and its elements. You then created a website root folder in which to store all of your pages and supporting files. Then you created web pages and filled them with content and images. You applied tables of information and imported content from other sources. You then sought reusable content and created a template from which you created other pages. Finally, you validated your sight elements and transferred them to a remote web server.

What's Next?

There's more to Dreamweaver, much more. In *Adobe® Dreamweaver® CS6: Part 2*, you will create pages with many more niceties for your site visitor. You will learn how to use Flash CS6 animations and video on your site. You will practice the more complex capabilities of CSS and HTML 5.0 while integrating and maximizing the creative power of Dreamweaver CS6. You will also learn to utilize the Multiscreen Preview of Dreamweaver CS6 for anticipating how your pages will appear on phones, tablets, and desktop devices.

You are encouraged to explore Dreamweaver further by actively participating in any of the social media forums set up by your instructor or training administrator through the **Social Media** tile on the LogicalCHOICE Course screen.

Customizing the Workspace

Appendix Introduction

As you become more comfortable with the Dreamweaver interface, you may want to modify some elements to provide a more convenient environment in which to work. The Dreamweaver workspace is an integrated group consisting of the document window, the **Application** bar, the **Properties** panel, and panel groups. The arrangement of these elements makes for workspaces that can be more convenient for you. In addition, you may resize any area at any time to provide more space. The adjacent areas will readjust.

TOPIC A

Predefined Workspaces

Dreamweaver provides a number of workspaces that contain windows and panels organized in a suitable manner for you to work. You have two advantages with these workspaces. You can rearrange the components of the workspace at any time and you can return them to their original layout quickly.

Workspaces

There are eight pre-configured workspace layouts. They are designed for the various contributors to web pages. With each workspace, panels important to the contributor are placed in a prominent position so they are convenient. The workspaces are named according to the type of task. They can be rearranged and saved with a new name and they can be restored to their original configuration.

Figure A-1: The Workspace drop-down menu.

Panels and Panel Groups

Panels are listed in the **Window** menu. Any panel you need that is not currently opened can be opened from the **Window** menu. With the exception of the **Properties** panel, which is generally placed at the bottom right of the screen, other panels are displayed to the right of the screen singularly or in groups. Every panel has a tab. If a panel is open, double-clicking on the tab will collapse it. If the panel is closed (just the tab showing), selecting the tab will open the panel. By right-clicking on any panel tab, you can collapse the panels to icons, releasing space for your work area. Finally, panels can be dragged free into floating panels and they can be returned to the collection of panels to the right of the workspace. Restoring the workspace is done easily by using the **Workspace** drop-down list.

Caution: Floating or loose panels can be troublesome because they cover areas of the workspace. They are also challenging to return to the panel area on the right. You should explore floating panels if you are working with a large monitor or two monitors where floating panels can be moved to a convenient location and not get in the way of your documents. Also, it is best to become familiar with Dreamweaver before floating panels.

The Dock

The *dock* is the area to the right of the screen where the panels are normally displayed. Panels can be docked alone or in panel groups. If you are returning a panel to the dock, look for the blue line indicating where the panel will be placed when you release the mouse button.

Panel Rearrangement

Feel free to relocate a panel for your convenience. If you have a large monitor or you are working with two monitors, placing a panel out of the way is especially convenient. Panels can be returned to their original location by dragging them back or restoring the workspace.

If you find an expedient workspace arrangement after moving the location of some panels, you can save it as a new workspace with a new name and return to it at any time by choosing it from the **Workspace** drop-down menu.

Customize the Personalized Workspace Layouts

From time to time you should view the various workspaces Dreamweaver offers. You can do this by using the **Workspace** drop-down menu. After relocating the panels you use the most, you can save the newly customized workspace layout with a new name.

Preferences

The Dreamweaver environment can be controlled further with an extensive choice of preferences. The preferences dialog box presents 19 categories of preferences. The general purpose for each category is listed in the table.

Category	Preference Options
General	Document, start up, editing options, number of history steps kept, and spelling dictionary
Accessibility	Showing accessibility attributes for page elements
AP Elements	Default attributes for absolutely positioned elements (<div>s)
Code Coloring	Color choices for coloring code text
Code Format	Rules and syntax for indents, tabs, code, tags, attributes, and styles
Code Hints	Rules for automatic completion of tags and tag selection drop-down menus
Code Rewriting	Rules for correcting code
Copy / Paste	Defaults for pasting text copied from other sources including Microsoft Word
CSS Styles	Defaults for using shorthand CSS rules and choice of where to edit CSS rules
File Compare	Identify and set location of a file comparison application (not supplied)
File Types / Editors	File types to be opened in the default editor and internal editors to be used (An external editor can be named if preferred.)

Category	Preference Options
Fonts	Default proportional and fixed fonts for web pages and font for the code window
Highlighting	Color highlighting for page regions, library items, live data, and mouse overs
Invisible Elements	Invisible elements to be marked with yellow icons
New Document	Default new document description including type, default extension and encoding
Preview in Browser	List of testing browsers resident on computer (Browsers may be added.); designation of the primary and secondary browsers used
Site	Rules for displaying local files in expanded view, prompts for dependent files, FTP options, proxy host options, save before put choice, and prompt before moving files on server choice
W3C Validator	Default document type to which validation is performed and options to display errors and warnings
Window Sizes	Default window (web page) sizes for phones, tablets, and desktops and connection speed used to calculate time to download pages being constructed

Icons

Dreamweaver displays icons in grayscale but they can be displayed in color. If you prefer to see the icons in color in the **View** menu, select **Color Icons**.

Apply a Pre-configured Workspace Layout

To apply a pre-configured workspace layout:

1. To the right of the **Application** bar, select the **Workspace** drop-down `Designer ▾` arrow.
2. Choose the desired workspace layout.
3. Note the arrangement of elements.

Customize the Personalized Workspace Layout

To customize the personalized workspace layout:

1. Select **Window→[The Panel of Your Choice]** to display it.
2. Repeat step 1 if there are other panels to display.
3. Move the panels you use the most to a convenient location or to a panel group.
4. Right-click the tab of a panel or panel group you wish to remove.
5. Select **Close** or **Close Tab Group**.
6. To the right of the **Application** bar, select the **Workspace** drop-down arrow.
7. Select **New Workspace**.
8. Type the name of your new workspace.
9. Select **OK**.

Modify Preferences

To modify a preference:

1. Select **Edit→Preferences**.
2. In the **Preferences** dialog box, select the category you wish.

3. Select the options you wish, deselect the options you do not want, and add the choices desired.
4. Select **OK**.

Collapse Panels to Icons

To collapse panels to icons:

1. Right-click on any panel tab.
2. Select **Collapse to Icons**.
3. Note that the panels are reduced to icons and are taking up less space.

ACTIVITY A–1
Customizing Personalized Workspace Layout

Before You Begin

Dreamweaver is open.

Scenario

You have been working with Dreamweaver for some time and you would like to modify your workspace to make it more convenient.

1. Determine a workspace with which to begin and modify it.
   a) To the right of the **Application** bar, select the **Workspace** drop-down arrow.
   b) Select various workspaces and note the arrangement. Think about how convenient it would be to use them.
   c) Select the **Designer** workspace.
   d) Right-click the **Adobe Browser Lab** panel tab.
   e) Select **Close**.
   f) Right-click the **Business Catalyst** panel tab.
   g) Select **Close**.
   h) Select **Window→History**.
   i) On the **History** panel tab, click and drag it up and to the right of the **Insert** tab.
   j) When you see a blue line around the **Insert** panel release the mouse button.
   k) You created a panel group with the **Insert** panel and **History** panel sharing the same space in the dock.

2. Turn on color icons.
   a) Select **View→Color Icons**.
   b) Note that all icons are now colored.

3. Modify preferences
   a) Select **Edit→Preferences**.
   b) In the **Category** column, select **Fonts**.
   c) In the **Code view Size** drop-down list, select **12 pt (Medium)** and select **OK**.

4. Save the new workspace.
   a) To the right of the **Application** bar, select the **Workspace** drop-down arrow.
   b) Select **New Workspace**.
   c) Type *My Workspace* and select **OK**.
   d) Select the **Workspace** drop-down arrow and verify that **My Workspace** is listed and selected.
   e) Note that even if you rearrange this workspace, there is a menu choice to **Reset 'My Workspace'**.

B | Managing Copyrights and Citations

Appendix Introduction

All products resulting from human creativity are considered *intellectual property*. Copyright law, developed to protect intellectual property, was enacted to enable our society to progress. Because you create original work when you build web pages and you might use graphics, illustrations, and text created by others in building those pages, you are on both sides of the copyright law. As a web page creator, you seek both protection for your intellectual property and fair and legal use of the intellectual property of others.

TOPIC A

Copyrights and Usage

To function efficiently as a website creator, you must know and understand copyright and trademark laws.

Copyright Terminology

A *copyright* is protection of a specific and tangible expression of an idea. It does not protect the idea. That expression can take the form of a novel, song, design, movie, website, and so on. A trademark is similar but it protects a design, image, slogan, symbol, or word that identifies goods or services. The copyright owner obtains the copyright at the moment of realization or completion of the tangible result from the idea.

Copyright Notice

The use of a copyright notice was once required as a condition of copyright protection. However, it is now optional. The notice does not register the copyright with the U.S. Copyright Office. If you wish to register a copyright you must do it through that office.

It is a good idea to put a copyright notice on your website so visitors are reminded that your site is protected by copyright. The general form of the notice is "**Copyright 2014 The Emerald Epicure Ltd. All Rights Reserved.**" The copyright symbol © may be substituted for the word "**Copyright**."

Available Permissions for Use

One limitation to the copyright law is for fair use. Fair use allows limited use of a copyright-protected work. What is allowable is determined by the following factors:

* The purpose of the use
* The nature of the copyright-protected work
* How much is to be copied
* The effect on the market or value of the work

Fair use is determined on a case-by-case basis. It is in common use for commentary, criticism, library archiving, news reporting, research, scholarship, and teaching.

Citing for Proper Use

If you will be using text or graphics owned by others, you should properly cite the origin of the information. This should be done whether the copyright symbol or notice is present in the original or not.

Locating Copyright Holders

If you suspect a work is copyrighted, seek out the owner and request permission to use all or part of the work. Many websites have sufficient contact information. If you believe the copyright is recorded at the U.S. Copyright Office and it was recorded after 1978, you can research the owner online at **www.copyright.gov**. Copyrights recorded before 1978 can be researched by their staff for a fee.

C | Web Accessibility Standards

Appendix Introduction

Websites are visited by any number of people and the universal quality of the World Wide Web is that anyone who wishes to browse the WWW need only have access to a computer with a browser connected to the Internet. However, not everyone who comes to the WWW has full use of their vision, hearing, or hands. To make the WWW useful to everyone, here are suggestions and guidelines for helping those with difficulties to navigate and understand the content of your websites.

TOPIC A

Examine Web Accessability Standards

In this topic, you will examine web accessibility standards that may impact your Dreamweaver designs.

Section 508 Requirements

Section 508 was enacted by Congress in 1998 to amend the *Rehabilitation Act of 1973*. The purpose of Section 508 is to require federal agencies to make electronic and information technology accessible to people with disabilities. It doesn't require private websites to comply unless they are receiving federal funds or are operating under contract with a federal agency. However, the initiatives suggested in Section 508 are desirable. If complied with, they transfigure the WWW into a universal resource available to all. Because of the general acceptance of the guidelines those voluntary standards and guidelines are published by the World Wide Web Consortium (W3C) and the Web Accessibility Initiative (WAI).

Accessibility Standards

The W3C provides the *Web Content Accessibility Guidelines (WCAG)*, now in its second iteration and designated as WCAG 2.0. The guidelines are intended for practitioners functioning as web content developers (page authors, site designers, and so on), web authoring tool developers, web accessibility evaluation tool developers, and others who want or need a technical standard for web accessibility.

The recommendation is built around four principles that provide web accessibility. The principles suggest that web content should be perceivable, operable, understandable, and robust. Built around the four principles are 12 guidelines for which there are testable success criteria at three levels: A, AA, and AAA.

WCAG 2.0 Section	Principle	Description
1.1	Text Alternatives	Provide text alternatives for any non-text content so that it can be changed into other forms people need, such as large print, braille, speech, symbols, or simpler language.
1.2	Time-Based Media	Provide alternatives for time-based media.
1.3	Adaptable	Create content that can be presented in different ways (for example, simpler layout) without losing information or structure.
1.4	Distinguishable	Make it easier for users to see and hear content including separating foreground from background.
2.1	Keyboard Accessible	Make all functionality available from a keyboard.
2.2	Enough Time	Provide users enough time to read and use content.
2.3	Seizures	Do not design content in a way that is known to cause seizures.
2.4	Navigable	Provide ways to help users navigate, find content, and determine where they are.
3.1	Readable	Make text content readable and understandable.

WCAG 2.0 Section	Principle	Description
3.2	**Predictable**	Make web pages appear and operate in predictable ways.
3.3	**Input Assistance**	Help users avoid and correct mistakes.
4.1	**Compatible**	Maximize compatibility with current and future user agents, including assistive technologies.

This discussion of accessibility is an overview of the topic. In order for the practitioner to create web pages that comply with accessibility guidelines, it is essential that the W3C WCAG 2.0 recommendation be reviewed before applying its principles.

D Adobe Web Communication Using Dreamweaver CS6 Objectives

Selected Logical Operations courseware addresses the Adobe Web Communication Using Dreamweaver CS6 exam. The following table indicates where Dreamweaver CS6 Part 1 skills that are tested in the Adobe Web Communication Using Dreamweaver CS6 exam are covered.

Objective Domain	Covered In
Domain 1.0 Setting Project Requirements	
1.1 Identify the purpose, audience, and audience needs for a website.	Part 1, Topic 1-C, Topic 2-A
1.2 Identify web page content that is relevant to the website purpose and appropriate for the target audience.	Part 1, Topic 1-C, Topic 2-A
1.3 Demonstrate knowledge of standard copyright rules (related terms, obtaining permission, and citing copyrighted material).	Part 1, Topic 3-A, Appendix B
1.4 Demonstrate knowledge of website accessibility standards that address the needs of people with visual and motor impairments.	Part 1, Appendix C
1.5 Make website development decisions based on your analysis and interpretation of design specifications.	Part 1, Topic 1-C, Topic 2-A
1.6 Understand project management tasks and responsibilities.	Part 1, Topic 2-B
Domain 2.0 Planning Site Design and Page Layout	
2.1 Demonstrate general and Dreamweaver-specific knowledge of best practices for designing a website, such as maintaining consistency, separating content from design, using standard fonts, and utilizing visual hierarchy.	Part 1, Topic 1-C, Topic 2-A

Objective Domain	Covered In
2.2 Produce website designs that work equally well on various operating systems, browser versions/ configurations, and devices.	Part 1, Topic 9-A
2.3 Demonstrate knowledge of page layout design concepts and principles.	Part 1, Topic 2-B
2.4 Identify basic principles of website usability, readability, and accessibility.	Part 1, Topic 3-C, Topic 5-B, Appendix C
2.5 Demonstrate knowledge of flowcharts, storyboards, and wireframes to create web pages and a site map (site index) that maintain the planned website hierarchy.	Part 1, Topic 2-B
2.6 Communicate with others (such as peers and clients) about design plans.	Part 1, Topic 2-A
Domain 3.0 Understanding the Adobe Dreamweaver CS6 Interface	
3.1 Identify elements of the Dreamweaver interface.	Part 1, Topic 1-B
3.2 Use the Insert bar.	Part 1, Topic 1-B
3.3 Use the Property inspector.	Part 1, Topic 4-A
3.4 Use the Assets panel.	Part 1, Topic 7-A
3.5 Use the Files panel.	Part 1, Topic 1-B
3.6 Customize the workspace.	Part 1, Appendix A
Domain 4.0 Adding Content by Using Dreamweaver CS6	
4.1 Demonstrate knowledge of Hypertext Markup Language.	Part 1, Topic 1-A
4.2 Define a Dreamweaver site.	Part 1, Topic 2-C
4.3a Demonstrate knowledge of the steps used to create, save, and name a new HTML page.	Part 1, Topic 3-A
4.4 Add text to a web page.	Part 1, Topic 3-B
4.5 Insert images and apply alternative text on a web page.	Part 1, Topic 5-A
4.6 Link web content, using hyperlinks, e-mail links, and named anchors.	Part 1, Topics 8-A through 8-E
4.7 Include video and sound in a web page.	Part 2
4.8 Add animation and interactivity to content by using Adobe Flash and Adobe Edge.	Part 2
4.9 Insert navigation bars, rollover images, and buttons created in a drawing program on a web page.	Part 1, Topic 8-E
4.10 Build image maps.	Part 1, Topic 8-D
4.11 Import tabular data to a web page.	Part 1, Topic 6-B
4.12 Import and display a Microsoft Word or Microsoft Excel document to a web page.	Part 1, Topic 6-B

Objective Domain	Covered In
4.13 Create forms.	Part 2
Domain 5.0 Organizing Content by Using Dreamweaver CS6	
5.1 Set and modify document properties.	Part 2
5.2 Organize web page layout with relative and absolutely-positioned div tags and CSS styles.	Part 1, Topic 1-B, Topic 2-A, Topic 4-B
5.3 Modify text and text properties.	Part 1, Topic 3-B
5.4 Modify images and image properties.	Part 1, Topic 5-B
5.5 Create web page templates.	Part 1, Topic 7-C
5.6 Use basic HTML tags to set up an HTML document, format text, add links, create tables, and build ordered and unordered lists.	Part 1, Topic 4-A
5.7 Add head content to make a web page visible to search engines.	Part 1, Topic 3-B
5.8 Use CSS to implement a reusable design.	Part 1, Topic 4-A
Domain 6.0 Evaluating and Maintaining a Site by Using Dreamweaver CS6	
6.1 Conduct technical tests.	Part 2
6.2 Identify techniques for basic usability tests.	Part 2
6.3 Identify methods for collecting site feedback.	Part 1, Topic 2-A, Topic 8-B
6.4 Manage assets, links, and files for a site.	Part 1, Topic 7-A, Topics 8-A through 8-E
6.5 Publish and update site files to a remote server.	Part 1, Topic 9-B

Adobe Dreamweaver CS6 ACE Certification Exam Objectives

Selected Logical Operations courseware addresses Adobe Certified Expert (ACE) certification skills for Adobe Dreamweaver CS6. The following table indicates where Adobe Dreamweaver CS6 skills that map to Adobe Certified Expert (ACE) certification objectives are covered in the Logical Operations Adobe CS6 series of courses.

Objective Domain	Covered In
1.0 Navigating the workspace	
1.1 Working with the document window	
1.1.1 Understanding code view, split view, design view	Part 2
1.1.2 Adding a title in the Title field (where it appears and why)	Part 1, Topic 1-B
1.1.3 Difference between enabling Live view and Live code	Part 2
1.1.4 Refreshing Design view after updating code	Part 2
1.2 Managing files in the Files panel	
1.2.1 Understanding how to configure Files panel to sort files	Part 1,Topic 2-C
1.2.2 Using the options in the Files panel to choose/ manage sites	Part 2
1.3 Updating properties in the Property inspector	
1.3.1 Setting contextual options to affect selected elements	Part 1,Topic 1-B
1.3.2 Understanding HTML Vs. CSS sections of Property inspector	Part 1,Topic 1-B; Part 2
1.4 Configure workspace layout	
1.4.1 Applying the pre-configured workspace layouts	Appendix A
1.4.2 Customizing personalized workspace layouts	Appendix A
2.0 Defining a Site	
2.1 Creating the local root folder	
2.1.1 Understanding the concept of the site's local root folder	Part 1,Topic 2-C

Objective Domain	Covered In
2.2 Setting server information with hosting account details	
2.2.1 Adding new servers in the Site Setup dialog box	Part 2
2.2.2 Understanding connection via FTP Vs. Local/ Network	Part 2
2.2.3 Setting the root directory	Part 2
2.2.4 Enabling Passive FTP when working behind a firewall	Part 2
2.3 Connecting via FTP	
2.3.1 Testing the FTP connection to verify settings are correct	Part 2
3.0 Creating web pages	
3.1 Using the New Document dialog box	
3.1.1 Describing the basic file types Dreamweaver can create	Part 1,Topic 3-A
3.1.2 Setting the default page extension preference (.html or .htm)	Part 1,Topic 3-A
3.2 Creating and managing files with the Files Panel	
3.2.1 Understanding why pages must be saved in local root folder	Part 1,Topic 2-C
3.2.2 Organizing the hierarchy of files/folders to create site map	Part 1,Topic 2-B
3.2.3 Repositioning pages in the Files panel prevents broken links	Part 1,Topic 2-C
3.3 Previewing pages in a browser	
3.3.1 Setting the primary and secondary browsers	Part 1,Topic 1-B
3.3.2 Understanding the advantages of testing pages in a browser	Part 2
4.0 Laying out pages	
4.1 Using the layout section of the Insert Panel	
4.1.1 Understanding Div containers Vs. AP Divs	Part 1,Topic 1-B
4.1.2 Nesting Div containers	Part 1,Topic 4-A
4.1.3 Describing behavior of Div containers (expand to fit content)	Part 1,Topic 1-B
4.1.4 Advantages of Div containers Vs. using table cell layouts	Part 1,Topic 6-A
4.2 Creating fluid grid layouts	
4.2.1 Benefits of creating a fluid layout that targets 3 resolutions.	Part 2
4.2.2 Using the Insert panel to add new Fluid Grid Div containers	Part 2
4.2.3 Enabling Live view to define page region Div containers	Part 2

Objective Domain	Covered In
4.2.4 Using the Resolution Switcher to set/view each resolution	Part 2
4.2.5 Using the Multiscreen Preview panel to view simultaneously	Part 2
5.0 Adding and formatting text	
5.1 Inserting special characters	
5.1.1 Describing situations that require inserting special characters	Part 1,Topic 3-B
5.1.2 Understanding HTML encoding used for special characters	Part 1,Topic 3-B
5.2 Using Find and Replace	
5.2.1 Choosing search location (current page, folder, or entire site)	Part 2
5.2.2 Choosing type of content to find (text, source code, or tag)	Part 2
5.3 Using Spell Check	
5.3.1 Accessing and running the Check Spelling command	Part 1,Topic 9-A
5.4 Understanding paragraph and header tags	
5.4.1 Benefits of using the appropriate tags to contain text content	Part 1,Topic 3-B
5.4.2 Setting text format (P, H1, etc) in the Property inspector	Part 1,Topic 7-C
5.5 Inserting line breaks	
5.5.1 Understanding the difference between <p> and tags	Part 1,Topic 3-B
5.6 Creating lists	
5.6.1 Understanding 3 types of lists: bullet, numbered, definition	Part 1,Topic 3-C
5.6.2 Indenting list items in the Property inspector	Part 1,Topic 3-C
6.0 Working with Cascading Style Sheets (CSS)	
6.1 Understanding basic CSS syntax	
6.1.1 Describing 4 main selectors (Class, ID, Tag, and Compound)	Part 1,Topic 4-A; Part 2
6.1.2 Describing 3 locations for CSS (inline, HTML head, external)	Part 1,Topic 4-A
6.1.3 Understanding the cascade effect (which rules are applied)	Part 1,Topic 4-A
6.1.4 Understanding that CSS rules specify properties of elements	Part 1,Topic 4-A
6.1.5 Understanding that CSS can format and position page items	Part 1,Topic 4-B

Objective Domain	Covered In
6.1.6 Understanding the difference between margin and padding	Part 1,Topic 4-B
6.1.7 Setting color properties with hexadecimal values	Part 1,Topic 4-A
6.1.8 Using common CSS measurement values (%, pixel, and em)	Part 2
6.2 Creating and managing CSS styles in the CSS Styles panel.	
6.2.1 Linking an external CSS style sheet to a web page	Part 2
6.2.2 Creating a new CSS Style in the panel	Part 1,Topic 4-A
6.2.3 Editing a CSS style in the CSS Rule Definition dialog box	Part 1,Topic 5-A
6.2.4 Adding and deleting rules in the Properties pane	Part 1,Topic 3-A
6.3 Applying styles using the Property inspector	
6.3.1 Applying a style using the Target rule list in the CSS section	Part 1,Topic 3-A
6.3.2 Using the Edit style option in the CSS section	Part 1,Topic 2-B
6.3.3 Setting the Class of a selected element in the HTML section	Part 1,Topic 3-A
6.3.4 Setting the ID of a selected element in the HTML section	Part 1,Topic 3-A
7.0 Adding and managing Links	
7.1 Understanding basic link types	
7.1.1 Understanding that file:/// links are created in unsaved pages	Part 1,Topic 8-A
7.1.2 Describing relative, absolute, named anchor, and email links	Part 1,Topic 8-A; Part 2
7.1.3 Targeting blank (_blank) to open a link in a new window	Part 1,Topic 8-A
7.2 Creating links using the Property inspector	
7.2.1 Adding links: Link field, Point to File, or Browse for File	Part 1,Topic 8-A; Part 2
7.2.2 Adding a named anchor on the page	Part 1,Topic 8-B
7.2.3 Identifying default text link formatting (blue and underlined)	Part 1,Topic 8-A
7.2.4 Creating placeholder links with the # character	Part 1,Topic 8-B
7.3 Creating content navigation	
7.3.1 Understanding how to insert Spry Layout Objects (widgets)	Part 1,Topic 8-E; Part 2
7.3.2 Adding/deleting menu items and panels in the Property inspector	Part 1,Topic 8-E
7.3.3 Reordering menu items and panels in the Property inspector	Part 1,Topic 8-E

Objective Domain	Covered In
8.0 Adding images and rich media	
8.1 Inserting images	
8.1.1 Requirement of saving image files in the local root folder	Part 1,Topic 5-A
8.1.2 Inserting placeholder images while designing a site	Part 1,Topic 5-A
8.1.3 Inserting Rollover images	Part 1,Topic 8-E
8.1.4 Benefits of adding Alternate text for SEO and accessibility	Part 1,Topics 3-D, 5-A
8.1.5 Setting Align property to wrap images in text containers	Part 1,Topic 5-B
8.1.6 Understanding images should be at original size (don't scale)	Part 1,Topic 5-B
8.2 Using the Property inspector to update and edit images	
8.2.1 Understanding the crop, sharpen, brightness/contrast tools	Part 2
8.2.2 Using round-trip editing to launch external image editors	Part 2
8.3 Inserting Flash content	
8.3.1 Adding Flash animation and applications (SWF Files)	Part 2
8.3.2 Adding Flash video content (FLV files)	Part 2
9.0 Writing HTML code	
9.1 Using the Code view of the Document window	
9.1.1 Using the Wrap Tag option to edit HTML source code	Part 2
9.1.2 Collapsing and expanding selected sections of code	Part 2
9.1.3 Applying and removing comments	Part 2
9.1.4 Using code hints by typing <, /, or pressing the spacebar	Part 2
9.2 Making changes to code using Design view of the Document window	
9.2.1 Using Quick Tag Editor to insert or wrap code around a tag	Part 2
9.2.2 Right-clicking and choosing Edit Tag to invoke the dialog box	Part 2
9.3 Selecting specific code	
9.3.1 Working with the Code Navigator	Part 2
9.3.2 Using the Tag selector to select tags in a nested hierarchy	Part 2
9.3.3 Using Find and Replace to find a specific tag	Part 2
9.4 Understanding related files	

Objective Domain	Covered In
9.4.1 Types of related files: CSS, SSI, JavaScript, Spry data, XML	Part 2
9.4.2 Selecting related files by clicking tabs in Document window	Part 2
9.5 Working with behaviors	
9.5.1 Understanding behaviors (user interaction provokes action)	Part 2
9.5.2 Understanding events (onClick, onMouseOver, etc)	Part 2
9.5.3 Using the Tag Inspector panel to apply behaviors to tags	Part 2
9.5.4 Changing the order of applied behaviors	Part 2
9.5.5 Deleting behaviors previously applied to tags	Part 2
10.0 Working with templates and library items	
10.1 Creating and applying templates	
10.1.1 Understanding that templates contain common elements	Part 1, Topic 7-C
10.1.2 Creating new templates in New Document dialog box	Part 1, Topic 7-C
10.1.3 Creating pages from templates in New Document dialog box	Part 1, Topic 7-C
10.2 Inserting editable regions	
10.2.1 Inserting editable regions to define areas of page content	Part 1, Topic 7-C
10.3 Editing and updating templates	
10.3.1 Editing templates by opening up the DWT file directly	Part 1, Topic 7-C
10.3.2 Updating all pages that are based on an edited template	Part 1, Topic 7-C
10.4 Creating and editing Library items	
10.4.1 Understanding that Library items are reusable code chunks	Part 1, Topic 7-A
10.4.2 Using the New Document dialog box to create Library items	Part 1, Topic 7-A
10.4.3 Using the Assets panel to create Library items	Part 1, Topic 7-A
10.4.4 Editing Library items	Part 1, Topic 7-B
10.4.5 Inserting Library items	Part 1, Topic 7-A
11.0 Working with mobile devices	
11.1 Using jQuery Mobile	
11.1.1 Creating new jQuery Mobile files (New->Page from samples)	Part 2

Objective Domain	Covered In
11.1.2 Applying swatches with the jQuery Mobile Swatches panel	Part 2
11.2 Understanding PhoneGap	
11.2.1 Understanding that PhoneGap builds native apps for mobile	Part 2
11.2.2 Using PhoneGap Build Service panel to emulate mobile app	Part 2
11.2.3 Using PhoneGap Build Service to share app builds	Part 2
12.0 Launching a site	
12.1 Transferring files by using Get and Put	
12.1.1 Understanding the difference between Get and Put	Part 2
12.1.2 Choosing whether to upload dependent files	Part 2
12.2 Understanding and using Check In/Check Out	
12.2.1 Enabling Check In/Check Out in Advanced Site Setup dialog	Part 2
12.2.2 Using Check In/Check Out to enable team collaboration	Part 2
12.2.3 Overriding the Check Out feature to access locked files	Part 2
12.3 Uploading a site using the Files panel	
12.3.1 Understanding the differences between Remote and Local	Part 1, Topic 9-B
12.3.2 Expanding and collapsing the Files panel to see both panes	Part 2
12.3.3 Selecting the site's root folder to Put or Get the entire site	Part 2

Lesson Labs

Lesson labs are provided for certain lessons as additional learning resources for this course. Lesson labs are developed for selected lessons within a course in cases when they seem most instructionally useful as well as technically feasible. In general, labs are supplemental, optional unguided practice and may or may not be performed as part of the classroom activities. Your instructor will consider setup requirements, classroom timing, and instructional needs to determine which labs are appropriate for you to perform, and at what point during the class. If you do not perform the labs in class, your instructor can tell you if you can perform them independently as self-study, and if there are any special setup requirements.

Lesson Lab 1–1
Getting Started with Dreamweaver

Activity Time: 15 minutes

Data Files

C:\092001Data\Getting Started with Dreamweaver\festival.txt

C:\092001Data\Getting Started with Dreamweaver\graphics\bread_olives_oil.jpg

Scenario

You want to create another page with a graphic just to see how they go together.

---

1. Create a new page with the following attributes:
    *   **Blank Page**
    *   **Page Type: HTML**
    *   **Layout: 1 column, fixed, centered**
    *   Select **Create**

2. Add text content.
    a) Replace the title "Instructions" with *Olive Festivals*
    b) Delete all the remaining text.
    c) Add body text using the **festival.txt** file.

3. Change the background color to white.

4. Insert the **bread_olives_oil.jpg** graphic before the first paragraph.

5. Save and close the file.

Lesson Lab 3-1
Creating Web Pages

Activity Time: 15 minutes

Data File

C:\092001Data\Creating Web Pages\olive_glossary.txt

Scenario

You want to create an olive glossary page. You can use the definition list tags to do it.

---

1. Create a new page with the following attributes:
   - **Blank Page**
   - **Page Type: HTML**
   - **Layout: 1 column, fixed, centered**
   - Select **Create**

2. Add text content.
   a) Replace "Instructions" with *Olive Glossary*
   b) Delete all the remaining text.
   c) Switch to the **Code** view. Delete the text **<p> </p>** on line 16.
   d) Add all the text from the **olive_glossary.txt** file.

3. Format the definition list.
   a) Place the insertion point before the word "ACIDITY" in the area of line 16.
   b) Type **<dl><dt>** to begin the definition list and the first definition term.
   c) Place the insertion point after the word "ACIDITY."
   d) Type **</dt>** to end the first definition term.
   e) Place the insertion point before the words "Acidity is measured" in the paragraph.
   f) Type **<dd>** to begin the first definition data paragraph.
   g) Place the insertion point after the words "oleic acid content."
   h) Type **</dd>** to end the first definition data paragraph.
   i) Finally, place the insertion point after the text "becomes solid.</dd>."
   j) Type **</dl>** to end the definition list.
   k) Select the **Design** button.

4. Remove background color.

5. Save the file as *my_olive_glossary.html* and close all open files.

Lesson Lab 4–1
Using CSS

Activity Time: 15 minutes

Data Files

C:\092001Data\Using CSS\philosophy.html

C:\092001Data\Using CSS\graphics\texture_tile.png

Scenario

You created the company philosophy page some time ago and you want to style it by using CSS.

---

1. Apply a background texture to the **philosophy.html** page using the **texture_tile.png** file.

2. Add a border to the page.
   a) Set the **border-right** and **border-bottom** style as *solid #995544 5px*
   b) Set **border-top** and **border-left** style as *solid #d7ad7e 5px*

3. Save the file as *my_philosophy.html* and close it.

Lesson Lab 5–1
Inserting Images

Activity Time: 15 minutes

Data Files

C:\092001Data\Inserting Images\olive_venues.html

C:\092001Data\Inserting Images\graphics\spain_olives.jpg

C:\092001Data\Inserting Images\graphics\italy_olives.jpg

Scenario

Your olive venues page needs a couple of more pictures.

---

1. Open the **olive_venues.html** page and save it as *my_olive_venues.html*

2. Insert images into the file.
   a) Insert the image **spain_olives.jpg** before the text "It is the Romans…" with alternate text *Spanish Olive Growing Region* and resize the image, if necessary.
   b) Insert the image **italy_olives.jpg** before the text "Olive trees were not…" with alternate text *Olive Growing Region in Italy* and resize the image, if necessary.

3. Format the images.
   a) Format the **spain_olives.jpg** image so that it is left aligned.
   b) Format the **italy_olives.jpg** image so that it is right aligned.

4. Preview the page, then save and close all files.

Lesson Lab 6-1
Inserting Tables and Importing Content

Activity Time: 15 minutes

Data File

C:\092001Data\Inserting Tables and Importing Content\olive_countries.html

Scenario

You would like to construct a page by using a table.

---

1. Open the file and insert a table with the following specifications:
   - Rows: *3*
   - Columns: *3*
   - Table width: *950* pixels
   - Border thickness: *0*
   - Cell padding: *15*
   - Cell spacing: *5*
   - Header: None
   - Alignment: center

2. Move the page contents into the table so that it is formatted logically.

3. Restore the country names to headings with a **Heading 2** format.

4. Save the file as *my_olive_countries.html* and preview it in the browser. Then close all open files.

Lesson Lab 9–1
Sending the Website to the Web Server

Activity Time: 15 minutes

1. Which of the following are important validations of your site's contents?
   - ○ Checking the links, validating CSS, check spelling. and validating XHTML/HTML
   - ○ Validating CSS, validating XHTML/HTML, correcting grammar, and checking spelling
   - ○ Verifying colors, checking links, and validating CSS
   - ○ Validating XHTML/HTML, checking links, verifying templates, and validating CSS

2. When checking links, Dreamweaver discovers errors on which of the following?
   - ○ Misspelled text and double links
   - ○ Anchor links and files with email links
   - ○ External links and email links.
   - ○ Broken links and orphaned files

3. When considering the concept of accessibility, which reports are key?
   - ○ The Site Errors report and the Tasks Undone report
   - ○ The Broken Email report and the Missing reference report
   - ○ The Missing Alt Text report and the Untitled Documents report
   - ○ The Sequencing report and the Remote Server report

4. Which of the following are critical steps in uploading your site to the web server for the first time?
   - ○ Obtain connection information from your ISP or IT department.
   - ○ Have all of your site pages, graphics, and other supporting elements in your site root folder in Dreamweaver.
   - ○ Be sure your site has been set up in Dreamweaver.
   - ○ All of the above.

Solutions

ACTIVITY 2-2: Charting the Website

1. Of all the planning tools discussed, which planning tool do you consider the most important?

   A: Answers could include any or all of these elements: flow charts, wireframes, storyboards, site maps, and project management.

2. What components of a website require the most planning?

   A: Answers could include any or all of these elements: text, graphics, tables, navigation bars, side bars, and pages.

ACTIVITY 2-3: Setting Up a Website in Dreamweaver

5. Dreamweaver needs to know where you will be keeping your files for the website. That folder is called:
   - ○ Website folder
   - ○ Remote server folder
   - ◉ Local site folder
   - ○ Site files folder

6. The graphics folder holds the images used on the web pages. This folder should be stored:
   - ○ On the desktop.
   - ◉ In the site folder.
   - ○ Anywhere.
   - ○ On the server.

7. All of the following are considered site planning tools except:
   - ○ Storyboards
   - ○ Wireframes
   - ○ Flow charts
   - ◉ Dreamweaver

Lesson Lab 9-1: Sending the Website to the Web Server

1. Which of the following are important validations of your site's contents?
   - ⊙ Checking the links, validating CSS, check spelling. and validating XHTML/HTML
   - ○ Validating CSS, validating XHTML/HTML, correcting grammar, and checking spelling
   - ○ Verifying colors, checking links, and validating CSS
   - ○ Validating XHTML/HTML, checking links, verifying templates, and validating CSS

2. When checking links, Dreamweaver discovers errors on which of the following?
   - ○ Misspelled text and double links
   - ○ Anchor links and files with email links
   - ○ External links and email links.
   - ⊙ Broken links and orphaned files

3. When considering the concept of accessibility, which reports are key?
   - ○ The Site Errors report and the Tasks Undone report
   - ○ The Broken Email report and the Missing reference report
   - ⊙ The Missing Alt Text report and the Untitled Documents report
   - ○ The Sequencing report and the Remote Server report

4. Which of the following are critical steps in uploading your site to the web server for the first time?
   - ○ Obtain connection information from your ISP or IT department.
   - ○ Have all of your site pages, graphics, and other supporting elements in your site root folder in Dreamweaver.
   - ○ Be sure your site has been set up in Dreamweaver.
   - ⊙ All of the above.

Glossary

216 web safe colors
Default set of standard colors available in Dreamweaver color picker boxes. This set of colors was originally adopted because of limitations in computer monitors and graphics card capabilities. Web development is no longer limited to this set of colors.

Application bar
Element of the Dreamweaver user interface that contains Microsoft® Windows® menu commands and provides users with access to all Dreamweaver tools and commands.

banners
Colorful headings that display on a web page and that typically contain a logo or other graphic that reflects the purpose of a website.

class name
Identifying name assigned to a particular group of page elements used to apply uniform style to all group members.

copyright
Legal protection of the specific and tangible expression of an idea.

CSS
(Cascading Style Sheets) Styling system that allows web developers to apply elements of style to content on web pages.

DNS
(Domain Name Service) Internet utility that translates text-based domain name addresses into the numerical addresses used by computers.

dock
Element of the Dreamweaver user interface that displays various command panels.

Dreamweaver workspace
Virtual environment within Dreamweaver consisting of the document a user is working with, and all of Dreamweaver's menus, toolbars, and panels.

editable region
An area within a Dreamweaver template in which content can be placed or created.

email link
Type of hyperlink that launches a blank email form in the user's default email application with the destination email address already populated.

embedded style sheet
Type of template file that, when inserted into the head of a document, applies style and formatting to the whole document.

external links
Link from one web page or section of a web page within a website to another location outside the website.

flow charts
Graphical representations of particular workflows used in planning the design of a website.

FTP
(File Transfer Protocol) Standard used to transfer documents from one computer to another, often times used to send individual web pages to a host server.

head components
Administrative components of web pages that are generally not seen by site visitors. These contain information used by web browsers and search engines.

home page
The point of entry for a visitor to a website; the main page of a website that summarizes the site's content and provides navigation to other site pages.

hotspots
The clickable links that make up an image map.

HTML
(HyperText Markup Language) Language based on a set of standards that is used to format and display content on websites and other electronic publications.

HTML tags
Element of HTML that defines the placement and formatting of web page content.

hyperlinks
Shortened form of the term hypertext link.

hypertext links
Navigable links from one web page or section of a web page to another.

ID selectors
Identifying name assigned to one particular element on a web page for the purpose of applying style.

image map
Image that has been divided into two or more regions that a site visitor can click as links to other pages, websites, or content.

intellectual property
Non-physical asset, which can be legally protected, that is the result of an idea, an innovation, or a design.

internal link
Link from one web page or section of a web page to another within the same website.

IP address
(Internet Protocol address) Numerical address used to identify and locate the computer system hosting a particular website.

Java Script
Computer language that supports the interactivity of on-screen elements of web pages.

layouts
Set of templates used to create web pages in Dreamweaver. These templates provide users with web page structure, but not specific content.

meta tags
Tags containing information about a web page that are invoked by web browsers or read by search engines, such as keywords that assist with web searches.

navigation bars
Collections of buttons used as navigation commands for a website.

nested table
A table inserted into the cell of another table for the purpose of managing complex cell content.

project management
Process of controlling the planning, documentation, and development of a complex deliverable product or result.

Rehabilitation Act of 1973

Law that prohibits discrimination against persons with disabilities by the U.S. Federal government, its agencies, its contractors, and any organization receiving Federal funding.

rollover effects

Visual changes that occur to a button or command when a user points the mouse pointer at the button or command.

Section 508

Amendment to the Rehabilitation Act of 1973, which requires Federal agencies and private organizations that receive Federal funds to make electronic documents and related technology accessible to people with disabilities.

servers

On the World Wide Web, powerful computers that use HyperText Transfer Protocol to send Web pages to a requesting computer.

site maps

Master plan of a website, created during the design phase of website development, that displays all of the web pages a site will contain and how they are linked to each other.

storyboards

Detailed sketches of planned web pages, developed during the design phase, which are typically hand drawn.

templates

Pre-defined layouts for web pages that allow a user to create multiple web pages with similar structure.

URL

(Uniform Resource Locator) Standardized address, consisting of several distinct elements, used to identify a particular web-based resource.

WCAG

(Web Content Accessibility Guidelines) Set of recommendations, developed by the World Wide Web Consortium, for making web-based content accessible to persons with disabilities.

Web browser

Software application that allows users to search for and view web-based content.

web server

Powerful computer that both serves as a repository for the files that make up a website and provides a connection between a website and the World Wide Web.

welcome screen

The initial screen that displays when Dreamweaver launches. This screen contains links to all of the possible next steps for creating a website or opening an existing Dreamweaver project.

wireframes

Rough sketches of web page layouts used in the design phase of creating websites. These can include an indication of the type of content a page will contain, the location of the content and basic style elements, such as color.

XHTML

(eXtensible HyperText Markup Language) Variation of HTML that is based on eXtenisble Markup Language (XML). XHTML was adopted in an effort to distinguish content from elements of style.

XML

(eXtensible Markup Language) Language used to identify and transfer data to and from applications, computers, servers, and other destinations.

Index

092001S rev 2.1
ISBN - 13 978-1-4246-2001-2
ISBN - 10 1-4246-2001-5